Contents

Contents

Understand the Current Foreclosure Boom

The phone rings, but you know who it is. It's the same script as yesterday, and the day before, and the day before that. You know it as well as the dude at the other end of the line: "Is this _____ _____? How are you today? I'm calling for Little Apple Bank. This call is from a debt collector; any and all information obtained may be used to collect this debt. I'm calling about your home loan, which has a past due balance of _____. I need to know what your intentions are to pay this balance in full."

A table near the phone is full of bills—first notice, second notice, last notice. You've balanced one against the other in a desperate attempt to keep the wolves at bay. You face questions you never expected to have to ask: Which do you need more, the Internet connection or the cable TV? Health insurance or car insurance? New clothes or new glasses?

Among the bills are credit card checks, promises of relief. But you've already gone as far down that road as you can, and now you have $10,000, $20,000, $30,000 of consumer debt on top of your car loan and home mortgage. Just making the minimum payments is a stretch.

But above it all is your home. The world was full of so much promise when you bought it! You would grow with it, and it with you; its creaks and quirks worked their way into your subconscious, as your caring touches changed its "personality." To lose it now would be like losing a part of yourself. But the stack of bills bears witness: you have to do something, or you'll lose the home to foreclosure.

You Are Not Alone

Maybe your scenario isn't as bad as the one described above. Maybe you just lost your job, and the phone calls haven't started. Maybe you're waiting for a big payment and only need to hold off the lenders for a few months. Maybe you had an unexpected medical expense or someone defrauded you, and you suddenly find yourself $100,000 in debt. Or maybe you have a variable-interest loan, and the rates just went up and increased your monthly payments beyond your ability to pay.

Whatever the case, you're not alone. The tremendous increase in real estate values from 1997 to 2006—coupled with historically low interest rates—encouraged many, many people to buy more home than they could afford. After all, why not? You saw people around you gaining $20,000, $50,000, even $100,000 in home value every year without lifting a finger. If you're like many people currently experiencing foreclosure, you waited a few years before buying . . . and when prices kept rising, you finally felt you couldn't just stand back and watch. You needed a piece of the action.

Table 1.1. *Office of Federal Housing Enterprise Oversight (OFHEO) House Price Index*

Year	Appreciation	Year	Appreciation
1998	4.7%	2002	6.9%
1999	6.4%	2003	8.0%
2000	8.1%	2004	11.2%
2001	6.9%	2005	13.0%

I remember an open house I held back in 2002, when I was still a real estate agent in San Francisco. One guy came in, looked around with a smirk on his face, and finally came over to me. "It's a nice place," he said. "Too bad the housing market's about to crash." I listened, cornered, while he recited 20 minutes of the usual reasons: prices were out of line with income, the dot-com crash had ruined the local economy, people were leaving the city, and so on.

Of course, he might have been right. But he was way, way off in 2002. And when the market value of that $900,000 condo had risen to $1,300,000 by 2006, it was hard to continue making such arguments. According to the "House Price Index" published quarterly by the Office of Federal Housing Enterprise Oversight, or OFHEO (*www.ofheo.gov*), single-family houses nationwide appreciated by the average amounts shown in Table 1.1.

The easy way to money and security seemed clear: just buy, buy, buy. The more you buy, the richer you'll become. Certainly that was the chant of people "in the industry"—agents, mortgage brokers, title insurers, and the like. Wednesday-morning gatherings at my real estate agency were like revival meetings: How many people did we make rich this week by helping them buy homes? Excellent, excellent! At lunch with a mortgage broker one day, I said something about "when the market slows down," and he abruptly held up his hand to stop me. "We don't talk about that," he said. "We always stay positive." At the same time, ambitious buyers pressured even the most conservative real estate professionals to help them make ever more risky deals.

Rising values—and a newly active mortgage market—also enabled people who already had homes to do cash-out refinances to convert their increase in equity into cash in their pockets. Some did so strategically, figuring that they could increase their home's value by $50,000 with a $30,000 kitchen remodel. Others did so out of necessity due to life crises such as illness or job loss. Others did so for frivolous purchases. Whatever the case, there's no denying that the new availability of money was a great temptation—one that discouraged consideration of a possible downside.

The rush to buy or refinance led to "irrational exuberance," where borrowers scrambled to get any kinds of home loans they could. Three types of loans that were previously considered risky became commonplace.

Adjustable-rate loans. Adjustable-rate loans start out with a low interest rate for a predetermined period, typically three or five years, before rising. Borrowers needed only to qualify for an adjustable-rate loan at the lower initial rate, then lived on hope that they'd be able to afford the higher rate when it kicked in. Such loans gave them far more buying power than they would otherwise have had. For example, someone who would qualify for only $200,000 with a traditional 6.5 percent, fixed-rate loan would qualify for over $280,000 with an adjustable-rate loan of 3.5 percent. But at the end of that three or five years, the rate would "adjust" upwards; if it ended up at 6.5 percent, the monthly payment would go from $1,264 to $1,779. Woe to the homeowner who couldn't afford the extra $515 every month!

Interest-only loans. As with an adjustable-rate loan, the idea of an interest-only loan is to lower the monthly payment as much as possible, thereby increasing the amount of purchase money available to the homebuyer. Taking our example above of a $200,000 loan at 6.5 percent interest, the payment of $1,264 includes $1,083 of interest, with only $181 going toward the amount owed, or principal. (We'll examine loan math in Chapter 6, "Understand Your Loan.") So a 6.5 percent loan where the interest *and* principal repayment is $1,264 monthly gives you $200,000 to play with. But what if the same $1,264 went only toward interest: How big would the loan be then? A few keystrokes on our calculator tell us that it's a little over $233,000 dollars. Voilà, you can buy a home that costs $33,000 more!

The downside to an interest-only loan is that you never actually repay it: you just maintain it at its current level. So at origination, you owe $233,000; in a year, you'll owe $233,000; and in 20 years, you'll still owe $233,000. That's fine if home values increase, as they (nearly) always have over the long run. The problem emerges if home values go down. Because you haven't been paying off the loan, every penny of lost value comes out of your deposit. If you put $40,000 down to buy your home, you might find that selling it and repaying the $233,000 loan gives you only $10,000, or nothing—or even less than nothing, if the value's dropped more than the size of your deposit. In some states, you might even have to pay additional money to your lender when you lose your home. (See Chapter 10, "Face the Foreclosure Process," for details.)

Subprime and Alt-A loans. Lenders classify prospective loans into two main categories. The ones that are most likely to be paid off on time and in full are called prime, or A-paper. These loans have comparatively low interest rates and fees. Those that are riskier are called subprime, or B-paper.

These classifications are based on the qualifications of the borrowers, including their credit scores, income, existing debt level, and documentation, along with characteristics of the purchase (such as down payment size). A typical prime loan goes to someone with a FICO credit score over 700, a down payment of 20 percent or more of the purchase price, few debts, substantial cash reserves, a long-standing job that easily covers the mortgage payments, and documentation that proves all these things.

A third category, Alt-A, refers to loans given to borrowers who have credit scores good enough to qualify for a prime loan but who aren't able to document their earnings.

A Perfect Storm for Foreclosures

Rising home values allowed people who purchased with such loans before 2003 or 2004 to (mostly) escape bad consequences. To be sure, some were forced out of homes that were simply too expensive for them when adversity struck or their adjustable-rate loans reset. But they, unlike people who bought more recently, had options by the grace of their homes' increase in value. So what if Mr. and Mrs. Ramirez can't afford payments on the big home they bought for $400,000? It's now worth $500,000; they can sell it, take the money, and buy something a little smaller. Or they can put the money in the bank and rent a place for a few years until they're ready to buy again. Money might not buy happiness, but it can sure remove barriers to it. Recent increases in home values protected people from the deepest pains of foreclosure.

Then values stopped rising and even sagged a little. OFHEO's statistics showed an annual increase of only 1.8 percent in in the annual period ending September 2007, far below the 13.0 percent increase of 2005, and falling. Homebuyers whose optimism was fueled by previously increasing values started facing foreclosure. It's no surprise that three of the states with the greatest increase in home values—Nevada, California, and Florida—now top the foreclosure list. As I write this in December 2007, foreclosures across the United States have literally doubled from a year ago: according to the NeighborWorks Center for Foreclosure Solutions (*www.nw.org*), over 50,000 families *per month* now enter foreclosure.

So whatever your situation, don't feel bad. If you made a mistake, it was at least an understandable one, given the information you had at the time. The point now is to accept things as they are and move forward in the best way possible. Your best chance at beating this thing comes from facing it. Don't panic, ignore the problem, or indulge in fantasy. Instead be truthful, make an intelligent plan, and execute it.

Memorize Five Essential Truths

Everything that follows in this book is based on five Essential Truths:

1. *You can't beat math.* There are few absolutes in the world: even gravity varies depending on where you stand. But one plus one equals two in every galaxy, and you'll never discharge a debt with payments of $100 per month when the interest is $125 per month.

   Mortgages are a game of numbers, so you'll have to do some math to figure out the size of the hole you're in—and how to get out. "Math anxiety" strikes fear in the hearts of millions of Americans. If you're one of them, don't worry. The math is fairly simple, can be done on a calculator, and usually only has to be done once per situation. If you can look at two numbers and tell which is bigger, you can do the math needed to get out of foreclosure.

2. *There is no magic bullet.* There's nothing more natural to the human condition than to wish for a sudden solution to difficult problems. In fact, you may discover resources you didn't know you had before you faced foreclosure, such as a rich uncle who's willing to help. But you're unlikely to find a suitcase full of money in the street—and even if you do, it may come with a curse (such as the attention of the gangster who lost it!). Your best way out of this is to make plans based on likelihoods, not fantasies, and your situation certainly won't get better unless you take steps to change it.

3. *You have options.* The parties involved in your loan—mortgagees or note holders, other creditors, government bodies, credit counselors, and, of course, you—represent a huge spectrum of motivations, perspectives, and ways of measuring

success. And they're all *people,* just trying to act according to their best interests in handling your case.

For example, one lender might need money right away and want your whole loan paid off as soon as possible; another might prefer to let you keep the loan but on different terms. You gain options when you understand these many complicated and often conflicting personalities. Your aim is to give them what they want while satisfying your needs.

Some of this understanding comes from knowing what motivates parties to a loan and the procedures and language they use to get what they want. We'll go into possible workout scenarios and how to talk to your lender and others in Chapter 5, "Call for Help." You'll learn about options you hadn't known before, but that's only half the battle. You'll also have to consider options you previously thought of as off-limits.

4. *Benefits should always outweigh costs.* Too often in life, we go along doing what we've always done without examining whether our actions are worth the trouble. Gym memberships are a classic example: overwhelmingly, people keep renewing their memberships long after they've stopped using the facilities with the idea that "I'll start doing it again someday." The benefit they're getting for their $50 (or more) per month is the *ability* to go back and use the gym, even if they never actually take advantage of it. But most people only want to pay for services they use; that means taking a hard look at your life and eliminating costs that don't deliver benefits of equal value.

The problem with a pure *cost–benefit analysis* is that costs and benefits usually can't be reduced to numbers you can compare directly. For example, you could reduce food expenses by only eating ramen noodles and peanut butter—and many first-year college students do so. And just like those poor students, you'll soon find yourself exhausted and malnourished, missing appointments and tallying up doctor's bills that far outstrip the cost of an occasional vegetable. Some expenses (such as insurance) are gambles where the best you can do is play the percentages, while others (such as an annual trip to see your family) have benefits that simply can't be quantified.

Still, in facing your foreclosure, you need to be willing to expose every expense—and I mean *every* expense—to a cost-benefit analysis. Prime among them: What is the cost of keeping my home? What would be the cost of losing it? What benefits would I get in either case? Which leads us to . . .

5. *You'll have to face difficult realizations and make difficult decisions—but you will survive.* Foreclosure, like illness and divorce, forces you to take a hard look at yourself. Chances are, you've avoided looking at some crucial facts about your finances as you hoped against hope that you'd be able to make the mortgage work without big changes to your life.

It might be hard to believe now, but in the end, you might find that this crisis has enriched your life in ways you can't imagine. Many of us in the Silicon Valley area know people who struggled to keep up the high-priced lifestyle they got to know during the dot-com boom that ended in 2001. A lot of them came out of it with nice cars, expensive home electronics—and tens of thousands of dollars in debts they couldn't pay off because the high-paying contracts had dried up. One guy I know sold his car and dropped his gym membership . . . and then found that the two "losses" canceled each other out. He started riding his bike everywhere, getting in far better shape than he had from listlessly using the StairMaster once a week. Plus, he discovered parts of his neighborhood he'd never seen by car. You never know!

As for your survival: Before the mid-1800s, Americans who owed money could be thrown into debtors' prisons, where they were held until they somehow repaid their debts *plus* the costs of their imprisonment. (Robert Morris, who signed the Declaration of Independence and helped finance the Revolutionary War, died in poverty shortly after having spent four years in such a place.)

No matter what an overzealous collection agent tells you on the phone, you're not going to jail simply because of your foreclosure. Your quality of life might drop, you might have to sell precious family heirlooms or face personal embarrassments, and you might be repaying the debt for the rest of your life. But although the Bankruptcy Abuse Prevention and Consumer Protection Act of 2005 (BAPCPA) has made life a lot tougher for people struggling their way out of foreclosure, it still allows for means testing to protect you from absolute destitution. You might even walk away from your foreclosure with some money in your pocket! If so, you'll be better off than the millions of American renters who lose their homes to eviction every year with nothing to show for it.

Move Forward

The inscription "Know Thyself" welcomed truth-seekers to the temple of Apollo at Delphi in ancient Greece. As you'll see in upcoming chapters, that advice is as relevant today as it was thousands of years ago, as many steps to avoid foreclosure involve a close examination of your current situation. Knowledge of—and documentation supporting—your true financial situation will be required by lenders, counselors, and (should you go into foreclosure or bankruptcy) the courts. More importantly, this knowledge will give *you* confidence to move forward sure-footedly, with a realistic view of what's possible.

But enough preamble—let's get you out of foreclosure!

Get a Handle on Your Situation

The first step in escaping foreclosure is to collect all your relevant information in one place. If you're like most people, you have a vague idea of how much you owe and to whom. But the devil is in the details, and you'd be surprised at what comes out when you actually put it all together.

There are three steps to compiling your financial profile:

1. Set up a case file.

2. Find the information you need.

3. Put it in formats that are easy to manage and manipulate.

We'll look at each of these steps in turn.

Set Up a Case File

To set up a case file, you'll at least need some folders. If you're not familiar with your local stationery store, now's the time to pay it a visit! Humorist Mark Twain wrote, "The well-organized man can be comfortable anywhere, even in hell." A few dollars of well-chosen stationery supplies are worth many times their cost in the comfort and peace of mind they'll give you.

File folders come in three formats.

1. *Manila folder.* The first is the simple, folded piece of cardboard commonly known as a manila folder. These folders are slightly bigger than the legal (8½" × 14") or letter (8½" × 11") paper they're designed to contain, and tabs typically stick out from the top on which you can label the folder's contents.

2. *Hanging file folder.* These folders have metal reinforcements that allow them to hang from specially constructed frames.

3. *Accordion folder.* These folders have a securable flap on top that make them handy for carrying documents from place to place.

If you don't already have a filing cabinet, a simple box will do. The stationery store will have a wide variety: I recommend you get one *designed* for filing, with rails built in to hold hanging folders.

Filing systems are as personal and serious as religion to some people, and whichever one works for you is, by definition, the best. Personally, I put all my important papers in hanging folders in a standard, metal filing cabinet next to the fridge, and I have a smaller filing system right next to my desk for things I'm currently working on. I like hanging folders because their tops are all at the same height: manila folders too easily disappear when they bend and slip underneath each other inside a cabinet. Also, you can subdivide hanging folders by putting manila folders—which are slightly smaller—inside them. Whatever you do, be consistent, and label *everything*. If (like me) you have atrocious handwriting, buy a little labeling machine from the stationery store for $20 or $30.

Finally, clear space where you can store all your documents and work comfortably. It's true that paperwork doesn't need as much space as, say, fixing a car. But the space is no less important, and having a few extra square feet where you can set papers in piles can save you hours overall and prevent you from losing the one important file that someone demands later.

Maybe it seems silly to talk about filing folders and labeling machines when creditors are hounding you. But remember Essential Truth #2: There is no magic bullet. You're going to get out of this through a series of small, well-planned steps, not a giant leap. The ability to break down daunting challenges into easy-to-do tasks is called "deconstruction," and is the key to many of our species' greatest triumphs. In her book *Bird by Bird: Some Instructions on Writing and Life,* writer Anne Lamott described how her young brother, who had procrastinated on writing a school report about birds, managed to overcome the same feeling of helplessness you might feel now. Shortly before it was due, he broke down in tears and told his father that he was simply overwhelmed and was sure he couldn't have it done in time. His father sat him down, helped him set up his materials, and told him how to divide the report into pieces. So in the end it wasn't a big, mysterious, fearsome job: he just did it "bird by bird."

Example: The Lees' Story

You're now sitting in a comfortable chair at a well-organized desk, cup of tea (or whatever) by your side. Now it's time to stand up, stretch, take a deep breath, and find the information you'll need. If you've kept good files, you're already a step ahead; if not, don't fret. You might have to write some letters and make some phone calls to get everything you need, and you might even need to visit a notary public to prove that you are the person you say you are. Patience, cooperation, and time is all you need.

Obviously, every situation is different. For demonstration purposes we'll consider the scenario of a fictional couple named Pat and Jo Lee. Don't worry if you don't understand all the terms or if your situation is radically different: We're just after the basic concepts here.

Jo and Pat Lee live at 123 Home Street in Anytown, New York. Jo is a middle-school teacher with a gross annual income of $36,000 per year ($3,000 per month); Pat is a worker and part-owner at wholesale florist Fancy Flourishes, averaging $4,000/month in salary and profit sharing.

They purchased their home in January 2004 for $380,000 with two loans:

1. An adjustable-rate mortgage (ARM), fixed for the first three years and adjustable annually after that, for 80 percent of the purchase price ($304,000) with an initial interest rate of 2.9 percent (payment of $1,265/month), rising to 5.9 percent in January 2007. This increase raised their monthly payment by $486, to $1,751. The rate rose again to 6.9 percent in January 2008, so now their monthly payment for this loan is $1,924 per month. (We'll show

you how to calculate such figures in Chapter 6, "Understand Your Loan.")

2. A similar interest-only ARM for 15 percent of the purchase price ($57,000) with an initial interest rate of 4.9 percent ($233/month), adjusting to 7.9 percent in January 2007 ($375/month).

They were able to afford the payments, barely, until the rates reset in January 2007. Jo was due to get a large pay increase from the school district before then, but government cutbacks made it much smaller than expected. Making things worse, Pat was hit by a car in August 2007 and hasn't been able to work steadily since then. They'd been living for the last few months on Jo's salary, savings, and credit cards, but they're just about at the end of their ropes.

The property has appreciated at an average rate of about 3 percent per year and now has an estimated market value around $430,000.

Understand Why Lenders Need Your Financial Information

Lenders want answers to five questions, which all add up to one *big* question: How are we gonna get paid? You can remember the five questions with the acronym *DISCO*, which stands for *d*ebts, *i*ncome, *s*ecurity, *c*ircumstances, *o*we.

D: *What other debts and expenses do you have?* Your home loans only tell part of the story. If you're like most Americans, you also owe money that's not secured by your home, such as credit card debt or a car loan. Obviously, such debts and other expenses figure into your ability to keep paying the mortgage. If every month, you make $4,000 and have to pay out $3,500 for predictable expenses, you won't be able to keep up with a $1,000/month mortgage! (See Essential Truth #1: You can't beat math.)

I: *What is your* income *and asset profile?* What are your prospects for getting money? Lenders want to know not only how much you make but also how stable your income is, how long you've been making that much, whether you expect any changes in that amount, and so forth. If you have other ways of making money, that information will give them hope that your situation is only temporary, and they might be willing to wait before starting foreclosure proceedings. (See Chapter 5, "Call for Help.")

Your lender will also want you to look beyond your salary for financial resources. Do you own any valuable assets, such as jewels or vehicles? How about other real estate? Do you have investments that pay royalties or could be tapped for ready cash? Could friends or relatives help you get current on your loans? If you've got it, document it.

S: *How valuable is their* security—*that is, your home?* Ultimately, lenders have an "atom bomb" weapon in their arsenal: the ability to sell your home, take their money, and call it a day. But that bomb loses a lot of its force if sale of your home wouldn't get them all the money they're owed. That would be the case if the amount you owe on the house is greater than its worth.

How could that happen? Most commonly it's because (a) you borrowed more than your home was worth or (b) your home's value dropped below the loan amount. Sometimes a combination of both factors is involved. For example, let's say you borrowed $180,000 to buy a $200,000 home. The lender then gave you an additional line of credit for $15,000, which you used to pay off some debts; you now owe $195,000 on your $200,000 home. But then the town's major employer drastically cut its workforce, sharply reducing demand for homes in your area and lowering the value of your home to $190,000. You now owe $195,000 on a home that's worth $190,000. You are, as they say in the business, upside down. Even if the lender foreclosed on your home and sold it off, it would still lose $5,000. (In reality, it would lose a lot more than that, because costs of sale can total as much as 10 percent of a home's market value, as we'll discuss in Chapter 8, "Sell Before the Pain Starts".) In such a situation, lenders are more willing to help you work out a way to stay in your home. Simply put, they don't want it! They'd rather that it stay in your hands—at least until it's once again worth more than you owe.

If you've owned your home for more than a few years, it's probably gone up in value overall since you bought it, and you've probably also paid off some of the debt. Therefore, its sale *would* allow you to pay the lender everything that's owed and possibly have a little left over (assuming you haven't taken out more loans). The difference between the amount you owe on a home and its current value on the market is called gross equity; including all costs of sale gives you the net equity, or simply equity. Put simply, equity is the amount of money you'd walk away with if you sold your home. If you owe $200,000 on a home worth $300,000 and the costs of sale are $25,000, then you have $300,000 − $200,000 = $100,000 in gross equity, and $100,000 − $25,000 = $75,000 in net equity. In our example above, your gross equity is $190,000 − $195,000 = −$5,000; that is, negative equity.

C: _Are there any other_ circumstances _to consider?_ Maybe you're facing foreclosure because of a personal disaster, such as illness, accident, or loss of your assets or job. Maybe that disaster seems overwhelming to you. In a country where hospital bills and long-term care can easily add up to hundreds of thousands of dollars, how could any ordinary person hope to get above water again?

Now's a good time to remember Essential Truth #3: You have options. You look at that $300,000 hospital bill and despair of ever paying it off, but a lender might dispassionately sit down with a calculator and decide that you _will_ be able to pay off both the mortgage and the bill over time and make a deal with you. (Isn't it inspiring when the clear eyes of others see potential in you that's evaded your own vision?)

O: _How much money do you_ owe _on your home?_ One of the first things a lender will do if you enter foreclosure is to go to the local county recorder's office to see what encumbrances have been placed against your home. Put simply, an encumbrance is anything that reduces your rights of ownership (not including common matters that affect every property, such as laws that deprive you of the "right" to set fire to the place.) Encumbrances can be either monetary or nonmonetary. Monetary encumbrances, also known as liens, say, "You're obliged to pay this much money to such-and-such person, or you'll lose your property." Nonmonetary encumbrances, such as easements, affect what you're allowed to do with your property, and because they don't typically figure into foreclosure matters, we won't be looking at them.

Encumbrances can be voluntary (you chose to put them on your property) or involuntary (they were forced on you, such as a judgment from a lost lawsuit). Many states have laws that protect equity in your home from being taken and sold by involuntary creditors, such as people who trip and fall on your property: discussion of this topic is outside this book's scope.

Mortgages are monetary, voluntary encumbrances and are recorded with the county recorder's office soon after you sign them. (You might remember having to sign mortgage papers in front of a notary public. Some of those went straight from the signing office to the recorder's office.) This government office maintains files of recorded documents relating to every parcel of property in its jurisdiction. So when people do a title search, they learn about all recorded encumbrances, including loans you took out that were secured by your home.

You can do a title search on your own home either by going to the recorder's office yourself or by getting a professional to do it for you. (Who that professional is depends on where you live. In some states, title searches are done by title companies set up for that purpose, while in others, they're done by lawyers and their staffs.) It's now also possible to order title searches online, for example through TitleSearch.com (*www.titlesearch.com*).

This information, together with a guess at the value of your home, helps lenders and other stakeholders decide how they want to handle your case. Approaching them with all this information up front shows that you understand your situation and are ready to deal.

Gather the Documents You'll Need

With DISCO as a guide, we can come up with a checklist of documents for your case file. (Skip those that don't apply to you, of course.)

Debts and expenses.

- *The latest statements from all your vehicle loans.* Can't find yours? Call the car loan company. If you don't remember who that is, then assuming you bought the car from a dealership, look at the contract you signed when you bought it or contact the dealer. Contact information for the lender, or "lienholder," should appear on the contract.

- *The latest statements from all your credit cards.* Don't have them? No problem: call the phone number on the back of each card and ask for a new copy to be mailed to you. As with most requests for financial information, you'll have to provide some proof of identity, such as your mother's maiden name.

- *Statements from any other debts, such as student loans.* Technically, lenders might only ask for evidence of long-term debts—that is, those that have lasted at least a year or are expected to last that long. But this is no time to equivocate. You *want* them to see your true financial picture, warts and all. Hiding debts from them isn't going to make the money suddenly appear, but it might lead them to think that you don't need as much help as you really do. Show them everything.

Income and asset profile.

- *Federal income tax filings from the last two years.* If you didn't keep one (for shame!), you can request complete copies from the government by filing the Internal Revenue Service's Form 4506, "Request for Copy of Tax Return," which you can download from *www.irs.gov/pub/irs-pdf/f4506.pdf.* The return costs $39 per year requested and takes up to 60 days to arrive. But here's a trick: at this point, you only need a "Transcript of Tax Return," which shows printouts of relevant figures from your tax return rather than the full thing. It's free and takes only two weeks to arrive. Get the transcript by filing Form 4506-T (*www.irs.gov/pub/irs-pdf/f4506t.pdf*).

■ *Other tax documents from your businesses.* These include Schedule Cs ("Profit or Loss from Business—Sole Proprietorship") for businesses you run without partners and Forms 1065 ("U.S. Partnership Return of Income") and Schedule K-1s ("Partner's Share of Income, Credits, Deductions, etc.") from any partnerships you have. For corporations, include W-2 forms for all employees, Forms 1120 ("U.S. Corporation Income Tax Return") or 1120-S for S corporations, and Forms 2106 ("Employee Business Expenses").

■ *The last two months of pay stubs* or other documents that show how much money you currently make. This can get tricky if you're currently unemployed: How will they know how much money you're capable of making? One way is to collect old evidence of earnings, such as W-2 forms (statements showing the year's salary and deductions at a given job), 1099 forms (for nonsalaried earnings, such as for contractors), and pay stubs from jobs you no longer hold. Ideally, you'll be able to show a history of making enough money to pay your mortgage. It's hard for lenders to believe that you'll be able to solve your problems by suddenly making more than you ever have.

■ *Profit and loss statements* from any businesses in which you're involved. If you haven't kept an organized profit and loss statement for your business, past tax filings—and any other financial records you have—will help you create one. This is a much bigger job than can be addressed in this book. A Certified Public Accountant (CPA) can help you through the process.

■ *Recent bank statements.* More and more, banks and other financial institutions have been encouraging their members to accept "paperless statements"—that is, to get information about their accounts online or via the phone. However, they have to give you printed copies of past statements when you request them, although they might charge you for the privilege. Call or visit your bank to find out. If you already do your banking online, then you can just log on and print out old statements.

■ *A list of valuable assets other than equity in your home.* As shown in Table 2.1, this can be a simple list with three columns: a brief name for the item, its description, and the likely value that it would fetch at a sale. It's tempting to overestimate the value of your assets—hey, you paid $20,000 for that car and took really good care of it! But if all the other classified ads ask only $8,000 for the same car from the same year with the same mileage, you're not going to do much better. (Economists call this the principle of substitution, which states that the value of an item is set by the cost of other items that could perfectly substitute for it.)

You can get a realistic estimate of vehicle value by consulting a "blue book" designed for that purpose. For cars, a popular guide is the *Kelley Blue Book* (*www.kbb.com*); for aircraft, it's *Aircraft Bluebook* (*www.aircraftbluebook.com*); and for boats and RVs, *NADA Guides* (*www.nadaguides.com*). For just about everything else, do a search for items similar to yours on the online auction

Table 2.1. *Sample List of Assets*

Name of Asset	Description	Value
Jo's car	2001 Acura Integra, VIN 19UUA655Q1A000001, paid off	$10,000
Pat's car	1999 Ford F150 Pickup, VIN 2FTRX18W1XCA00001, paid off	$7,000
Music instruments	Pat's collection of instruments, mostly Yamaha brasses	$6,000
Jewelry	Collection of diamond pieces, appraised 1995	$5,000
Stock	40 shares of Google, @ $648.54 (as of November 20, 2007)	$25,942
TOTAL VALUE		**$53,942**

house eBay (*www.ebay.com*); on the results screen, check the "Completed Listings" box and click the "Show Items" button. This second step is important, because you want to find out how much people are actually paying for items like yours; it doesn't do any good to know only the asking price!

Include anything that could quickly be turned into cash, such as any stocks, bonds, or other securities you hold, at its current value. Don't include your home itself: we'll get to that next.

Security in your home.

■ *An estimate of your home's market value.* From least to most accurate (and expensive), three ways of getting this are (1) through a computer-driven system called an automated valuation model (AVM); (2) through a Broker Price Opinion (BPO); or (3) through a full appraisal. You won't need anything as fancy as a BPO or appraisal at this point, and fortunately the Web is home to at least a half-dozen free AVM systems. Popular among them are these:

- Coldwell Banker's Home Value Estimator: *www.coldwell banker.com/real_estate/Home_Value_Estimator*
- Cyberhomes: *www.cyberhomes.com*
- Eppraisal: *www.eppraisal.com*
- Reply: *www.reply.com*
- Zillow: *www.zillow.com*

Print out pages that give estimates of your home value from any of these sites—or better yet, from all of them. It's a good idea also to print out supporting pages that show, for example, the price of recent home sales in your area. There's no need to print out all the demographic stuff about school systems, crime rates, and the like. That information is there for the benefit of homebuyers who want to know more about the area and isn't of interest to lenders.

Circumstances lenders should know.

■ *A letter of explanation, sometimes called a LOX,* with supporting documentation. Loan processors handle hundreds or even thousands of loans per year. The human condition being what it is, they're not long on the job before they see some truly heartbreaking stories cross their desks. After a while, they learn how to separate truth from bull, and, on a more positive note, they eventually get to see people overcome adversity to go on to pay off their loans.

Some common hardships of borrowers include:

- Death of a coborrower
- Loss of your main source of income
- Reduction of income caused by market changes
- Reduction in hours or loss of a second job
- Medical expenses from illness
- Medical expenses from an accident
- Inability to work due to medical reasons
- Inability to work due to being thrown in jail
- Expenses from poor planning, such as a sudden bill for unpaid income tax
- Other unexpected expenses, for example from divorce, death, fire, or natural disaster

As you might imagine, some of these reasons elicit more sympathy than others! But in the end, lenders' financial judgment, not sympathy, primarily dictates how they work with you to avoid foreclosure.

The letter should give the facts in a straightforward manner, indicating the nature of the problem and—more importantly—how it affects your ability to pay your mortgage. It may be hard to condense months of suffering into a few words but try not to get carried away with the details. Many people find it easier to dictate such a letter to a friend, who can then edit it down to its salient points. Figure 2.1 shows an example.

Owed money on your home loan.

■ *Your original loan documents.* If you don't have copies of these, of course you could get them from the lender. But

Figure 2.1. *Sample Letter of Explanation*

Jo and Pat Lee
123 Home Street, Anytown, NY 10000

December 29, 2007

Loss Mitigation Department, Home Mortgages
Little Apple Bank
1 Liberty Plaza, 56th Floor
New York, NY 10006

Dear Little Apple Bank:

I'm writing in regard to my loan (#123456ABC) with your bank and to provide details on an unusual circumstance that should be considered in reference to my file.

On August 24, 2007, at approximately 10:15 PM, I was struck by a car while crossing Main Street in Anytown, New York. A passerby called for an ambulance, which took me to a hospital where I was treated for a concussion and a broken leg. Copies of the police and hospital reports are enclosed.

My job as owner and manager of a three-person wholesale flower distributor requires driving a truck, making deliveries, and substantial other physical activity. As a result, I was unable to work for two weeks after the accident while my leg healed. A week after I did return, I started experiencing dizziness and nausea. Nonetheless, I attempted to keep working, until one day I fainted in the refrigerated storage unit. On the advice of my doctor, I've been undergoing a series of tests to determine the cause.

In the meantime, our business lost a major contract when my absence prevented us from fulfilling it. That contract had a gross value of $20,000 per month in sales, which equals a reduction in my personal income of approximately $1,500 per month.

Figure 2.1. *Sample Letter of Explanation (continued)*

Further, the dizziness and nausea have continued, putting in question our ability to continue the business and preventing me from taking other work.

While my insurance has mostly covered my medical bills, the loss of income has prevented me from staying current on my mortgage payment to you.

I trust that you'll take my situation into consideration, and I hope that we'll work out a solution that benefits both of us. Please don't hesitate to call or write if I could provide further information.

Sincerely,

[Signature]

Pat Lee

---

what if you don't want to talk with the lender until you've had a chance to gather and study all your documents? If your loan originated in the last few years, you might also be able to get copies from other parties involved in the loan, such as the mortgage broker, lawyer, or escrow officer. Laws vary, but in many states, such people are required by law to hold on to such papers for a certain number of years. They might charge you a fee for retrieval, however.

■ *Your most current mortgage statement(s) or, if you can get them, payoff demands.* A payoff demand, as the name implies, is a statement from the lender that says how much money you'd need to pay off the loan completely. You should be able to order such a statement for free from your lender, possibly through its website. However, financial institutions usually charge a $10–$25 fee to any third party (such as your lawyer) who tries to get it or if you ask for it to be delivered in certain ways, such as by fax. (A mortgage estoppel letter is another name for the same information but is more legalistic in form.)

▪ *Any other documents relating to debts secured by your home.* These could include mechanic's liens; judgments, or unpaid property taxes. A list of these obligations will show up on the report you receive from doing a title search, although some of the entries can be a bit confusing if you're not used to reading such reports. (For example, the list includes ordinary, recurring taxes and assessments that you don't need to document.)

Summarize Your Situation

Now you have a big stack of papers in front of you—in neatly labeled and alphabetized folders, of course! The next step is to organize it so that the information is easy to manage and manipulate.

I'm going to assume that you have a computer with Internet access or at least have a friend with one you can use. If not, I strongly recommend you get one. Everyone you talk to about your foreclosure will assume you have a computer and will direct you to resources, such as websites, programs, and email, that are only available that way. New computers, with a screen and printer, cost as little as $500 these days; a knowledgeable friend can usually find a used one for $100 or less. Useful software programs such as FileMaker Pro and Microsoft Excel cost additional hundreds of dollars, but similar programs exist that will get the job done for free (such as Open Office at *www.openoffice.org*). If you can't buy a computer, you may be able to use one for free at a local library; a $20 "thumb drive," also called a "flash drive," lets you save your files for later use.

Balance Sheet

It's hard to have an at-a-glance idea of your financial situation when you have to shuffle around dozens of papers, so we're going to compress all the numbers into a balance sheet, which is a simple listing of assets (what you have) and liabilities (what you owe). Subtracting total liabilities from total assets gives you your net worth—the amount of money you could theoretically put in your pocket if you sold everything and paid off all the money you owe. Table 2.2 shows Pat and Jo Lee's balance sheet.

One item is of particular interest: the business loan made to a friend. Such debts *are* assets, but of course they're not the same as money in hand. You should discount them by some amount to make up for the risk of noncollection, in this case 50 percent. You might even be able to immediately sell that promissory note to a third party, such as a friend or a finance company. This is a common practice in the finance and business world, where it's called debt factoring, and is typically used for unpaid invoices. Determining the right discount rate and finding ways to monetize those accounts receivable are complicated issues, however, and well beyond the scope of this book.

If you've gotten this far, you might actually be breathing a sigh of relief that things aren't as bad as the bills alone would suggest. People often fail to realize the extent of financial wealth in their lives—if only it could be turned into money. Of course, converting possessions into cash to pay off a debt is emotionally painful,

Table 2.2. *Sample Balance Sheet*

Unless otherwise noted, all values are as of November 20, 2007.

Assets

Market value of real estate at 123 Home Street, Anytown, NY, per cyberhomes.com	$430,000
Jo's car (2001 Acura Integra, estimated market value per Kelley Blue Book), owned outright	$10,000
Pat's car (1999 Ford F150 pickup, estimated market value per Kelley Blue Book), owned outright	$7,000
Music instruments (collection of brasses, estimated value, not appraised)	$6,000
Jewelry (mostly diamond pieces, appraised 1995)	$5,000
Google stock (40 shares @$648.54 each)	$25,942
Joint bank account, Jo and Pat, Citibank #960-418001	$3,430
Share of wholesale flower business (Flourishing Fancies), estimated value	$40,000
Unsecured promissory note for business loan for $5,000 made to Dorothy Lightship, due January 1, 2009, discounted 50%	$2,500
TOTAL ASSETS	**$529,872**

Liabilities

1st mortgage on 123 Home Street, Anytown, NY, Little Apple Bank #12345678	$278,378
2nd mortgage on 123 Home Street, Anytown, NY, Little Apple Bank #87654	$57,000
Jo's Wachovia credit card, #1111 2222 3333 4567	$6,732

Table 2.2. *Sample Balance Sheet (continued)*

Pat's Citibank credit card, #2222 3333 4444 5678	$4,791
Jo's college loan, Happy Student Lenders #18841276	$53,162
Medical bills from Pat's recent accident	$783
TOTAL LIABILITIES	**$400,846**
Total assets	$529,872
Total liabilities	−$400,846
NET WORTH	**$129,026**

often causes hardship, and sometimes simply isn't possible. (In our example above, selling both cars might prevent everyone in the family from making a living!) Your job right now is just to lay it all on the table; you won't know what's possible until you consider the impossible. (Or as poet William Blake put it, "You never know what is enough unless you know what is more than enough.")

Budget

Next, you're going to look at your monthly budget. Once again, consider every current, reliable source of income and every major expense. Small entries—say, those under $100 per month—can be lumped together for simplicity, as in the "Misc. Household" entry in Table 2.3. As you can see, the monthly budget is set up very much like the balance sheet.

Table 2.3. *Sample Monthly Budget*

Unless otherwise noted, all amounts are estimates based on an average of monthly expenses over the past year, with adjustments as needed.

Income

Item	Description	Monthly Amount
Jo's salary	Middle-school teacher, Anytown school district	$3,000
Pat's salary & profit sharing	Fancy Flourishes owner and manager	$4,000
Other income	Interest, dividends, gifts, and refunds	$100
TOTAL MONTHLY INCOME		**$7,100**

Expenses

Item	Description	Monthly Amount
1st mortgage	Little Apple Bank #12345678, @6.9% (rate starting Jan. 2008)	$1,924
2nd mortgage	Little Apple Bank #87654, interest-only @7.9% (rate starting Jan. 2008)	$375
Property taxes	3.2% per year of assessed value of $362,000	$965
Property insurance	Watching Your Back (WYB) Insurers, Policy #321654	$150
Property maintenance	Estimated; includes savings for major expenditures	$100
Car insurance, Pat	1999 Ford F150, WYB Policy #77778888	$75
Car insurance, Jo	2001 Acura Integra, WYB Policy #55556666	$90

Table 2.3. *Sample Monthly Budget (continued)*

Item	Description	Monthly Amount
Pat's health insurance	WYB Policy #A987B654	$125
Jo's income taxes	Estimated, based on 28% of gross salary	$700
Pat's income taxes	Estimated, based on past year's income	$1,000
Jo's Wachovia	Credit card, #1111 2222 3333 4567; minimum payment	$125
Pat's Citibank	Credit card, #2222 3333 4444 5678; minimum payment	$100
Jo's college loan	Happy Student Lenders #18841276	$350
Medical bills	From Pat's recent accident	$30
Food	Groceries and work lunches	$650
Utilities	Gas, electric, phone, Internet, water, garbage	$200
Entertainment	Dining, movies, travel, etc.	$500
Gifts and charity	For friends and nonprofits	$100
Clothing	For both Pat and Jo	$50
Misc. Household	Includes cleaning supplies, light bulbs, toiletries, etc.	$100

TOTAL MONTHLY EXPENSES $7,709

Total monthly income	$7,100
Total monthly expenses	−$7,709

MONTHLY BALANCE   −$609

This process has uncovered a problem that goes beyond Pat's accident: even with a stable income, the Lees would have a deficit of about $600 per month. They were able to get by for the first few years because of their loans' low introductory rates. January 2007 brought increases in their monthly loan payments totaling $628; January 2008 added another $173.

Move Forward

But even if the news is tough to take, we are better off now, because at least we know where we stand. The Lees might have already known that they were losing money each month, but they probably didn't know exactly how much. They knew that interest rate increases had affected them but weren't sure how much. And they were devastated by Pat's accident and its aftermath, although they hadn't put its impact into words. But now they realize how wealthy they are in assets, how sales of those assets would stave off foreclosure, and how much home they can really afford. They're ready to begin.

How about you?

Rework Your
Income and Expenses

They say the perfect fight is the one you can avoid. So it is with foreclosure. In a perfect world, wouldn't you suddenly find a way to pay your mortgage, thereby avoiding difficult discussions with lenders, accountants, and lawyers?

So even if you've gone over your finances, let's take one more look. Obviously, the biggest expenses are the meatiest targets: eliminating a single $500/month expense would have more effect than taking a bag lunch to work once a week. But don't discount small efforts! If forgoing that fast-food lunch saves $5 per week, and both you and your spouse or partner do it, you'll save over $40 per month—which in turn could pay for $5,500–$7,000 worth of mortgage. That's nothing to sneeze at! Likewise, small increases in income can make a big difference. But you're better off saving $40 per week than earning it through a second job for one reason: taxes. If you're in the 28 percent tax bracket, you'll only take home a little under $29 of that $40.

Table 3.1. *Sample Monthly Expenses (Sorted)*

Item	Monthly Amount
1st mortgage	$1,924
Pat's income taxes	$1,000
Property taxes	$965
Jo's income taxes	$700
Food	$650
Entertainment	$500
2nd mortgage	$375
Jo's college loan	$350
Utilities	$200
Property insurance	$150
Property maintenance	$100
Pat's health insurance	$125
Jo's Wachovia credit card	$125
Pat's Citibank credit card	$100
Gifts and charity	$100
Misc. household	$100
Car insurance, Jo	$90
Car insurance, Pat	$75
Clothing	$50
Total Monthly Expenses	**$7,709**
Savings Goal (income minus expenses)	**$609**

So we'll take a look at expenses first, using our old friends, the Lees, as examples. To start, we'll look at their budget again but sorted so the biggest expenses are at the top, as in Table 3.1. (You can easily sort your own budget in a spreadsheet program or some word processors. Ask a friend for help if you don't know how, and remember to make a backup so you don't irreversibly undo your hard work.)

Interestingly, every number on this list *could* theoretically be lowered. But the goal isn't to cut to the bone, reduce every expense by a certain percentage, or make cuts that would cause unacceptable hardship. Rather, the idea is to at least *examine* each number with the idea of reduction in mind—and then to balance costs and benefits so you can make enough of a reduction with the least amount of pain.

However, there are four large categories of expense we won't examine now. We'll pass over possible savings in income taxes, because that's a whole other field of finance well beyond the scope of this book. And we'll delay discussion of lowering your mortgage itself until Chapter 5, "Call for Help." Thirdly, you can't go without property insurance, as you're required to carry insurance as a condition of your mortgages. Finally, there's really not much to do about property taxes except apply for a reassessment—a long-shot process that requires research, varies from county to county, and takes a long time.

That leaves us with three categories of expense:

1. *Discretionary expenses.* These are expenses that could be reduced by making changes in your day-to-day lifestyle. Generally speaking, they're also "scalable"; that is, a small lifestyle change will result in small savings, whereas a large lifestyle change will result in large savings. In this category fall six items on the list in Table 3.1 above: food,

entertainment, utilities, gifts and charity, misc. household, and clothing.

2. *Loan expenses.* Besides expenses related to their mortgages (which we'll discuss later), the Lees have three items of this type: two credit cards and a college loan.

3. *Recurring system support expenses.* This category includes expenses that are necessary to "keep things running," so to speak—for example, insurance and professional memberships. The only way to get rid of such expenses is to change or eliminate the system that requires them. Unlike scalable expenses such as gifts and clothing, you can't easily reduce your spending on them without some planning. In our example, Pat's health insurance wouldn't be necessary if Pat got rid of the flower distributorship and got a regular job that included health benefits, and neither Pat nor Jo's car insurance would be necessary if they sold their cars. They are also all-or-nothing discretionary costs: you have to either keep paying the whole expense or eliminate it entirely. (Property-related costs, such as insurance and maintenance also fall into this category, but obviously they don't figure into our plans—at least, not unless you ultimately decide to leave your home.)

Reduce Everyday Expenses

Discretionary expenses are what most people attack first when reducing their budgets. Unfortunately, they can also be the hardest to track, as they tend to be paid out-of-pocket, paid in cash, and paid in small amounts. Keeping in mind Essential Truth #4 (Benefits should always outweigh costs) you need accurate numbers to determine costs. There are two ways you can do that: either carry a small notebook and write down every penny that comes out of your pocket or pay for everything with a credit card. In either case, you'd have to scrutinize your records every month for a few months to get a clear picture of daily spending.

Quite frankly, few people have the discipline and organizational skills such record keeping requires. Still, it's worth trying for at least a few weeks—and it's not really that hard, once you get into the habit. Even if you can't ultimately find ways to cut back, just knowing where the money's going is enlightening.

Generally speaking, you can save money on *everything,* and there are dozens of books out there that can tell you how. The trade-offs are time and work. Take as an example the Lees' top discretionary expense (food). Restaurants are the most expensive way to eat, but in return for about $40 a day per person, you get three meals where you don't have to do anything except sit down and chew. Cafeteria-style meals are a bit cheaper because you have to walk the food to your table and the dishes to the trash; take-out food is cheaper still. In home cooking, prepared meals are pricier than their ingredients, and even ingredients themselves are on a price spectrum depending mostly on how much they've been processed.

At the cheap end, it's possible to eat nutritiously and well for under $5 per day, as many families do. All it takes is the time and effort to reconstitute beans, chop fruits and vegetables, boil rice, carve meat, and cook it all up. (The authors of the recent book *America's Cheapest Family* detail how they feed a family of *seven* well on a little over $10 per day.) While not everybody wants to cut back that much, the payoff can be enormous. The

$35/day saved on food between the top and bottom of the price ladder adds up to about $1,000/month for just one person. That's almost twice as much as the Lees need!

Such lifestyle changes require fundamental shifts in how you view yourself and your money—and you'll have to maintain these changes until you either find another source of income or another way to save money. But just looking at the numbers reminds us of Essential Truth #3: You have options, and Essential Truth #5: You'll have to face difficult realizations and make difficult decisions—but you will survive.

Moving on, we come to loan expenses. We'll focus on credit cards specifically, because they're more complicated than other types of long-term debt, such as student loans and car loans.

Review Consumer Credit Costs

But first things first: Do you know the interest rates you're paying on all your loans? If not, put down this book right now and find out. You should find this information on your latest bill or payment coupon; otherwise, you'll have to call the lender. But in any case you have a right to know.

At this point, it's worthwhile to review how interest rates work. You might already know all this, but a surprising number of people who carry debt don't really understand how much they're paying, or why, or how interest rates relate to monthly payments. Just in case you're among those many people, here's the deal.

Interest rates are given as a percentage of the amount owed. The word *percent* comes from the Latin word *cent,* meaning hundred, and in fact a percentage tells you how many parts per hundred something is.

When friends say they bought something at a 15 percent discount, that means they paid $15 less per every $100 of price. So if the item was priced at $300, they paid (3 × $100) – (3 × $15) for it, which equals $300 – $45 = $255.

Use percentages in math problems by dividing them by 100; i.e., by moving the decimal point two places to the left. So 15% = 0.15, 8.9% = 0.089, and 0.25% = 0.0025.

To figure out how much 15 percent is of an amount, multiply the amount by 0.15. So 15 percent of $100 is 0.15 × $100 = $15.

Similarly, 8.9 percent of $600 is 0.089 × $600 = $53.40 ... and so forth.

For credit cards, the percentage is annual for the amount of the debt. So let's say you charge $1,000 to a credit card that has a 12 percent interest rate. If you pay off the interest as it appears, you'll pay a total of $120 in interest charges, because $1,000 × 0.12 = $120.

To figure out the monthly rate, divide the yearly interest rate by 12 months. In this case, that's 0.12 / 12 = 0.01, or 1 percent per month. So you would pay $10 per month as interest on this $1,000 debt.

Things are actually a little more complicated than that, because the amount that's subject to interest changes as you either pay off or increase the amount that you owe. We'll talk about those complications in Chapter 6, "Understand Your Loan."

Table 3.2. *Sample Credit Card Statement Interest-Disclosure Section*

Type	Nominal APR	Periodic Rate	× Days	× Balance, This Rate	= Periodic Finance Charge
Purchases	14.020%	0.03841% (D)	32	$8,460.67	$103.99
Offer 5	3.990%	0.01093% (D)	32	$3,609.18	$12.62
Advance	23.020%	0.06307% (D)	32	$1,000.00	$20.18
Total Owed:				**$13,069.85**	
Total Finance Charge This Period:					**$136.79**

On car loans and student loans, you'll usually pay a basic, fixed interest rate for the entire loan amount. With credit card debt, however, you might find that you're paying a mixture of rates. Table 3.2 shows a few lines from the interest-disclosure section of an example credit card bill.

In this case, three interest rates are in play: 3.99 percent (hooray!), 14.02 percent (feh), and 23.02 percent (eek!). Credit card companies (and other lenders) figure out how much interest you have to pay by taking the annual percentage rate (APR) and dividing it by the 365 days in a year to get the periodic rate—that is, the rate you're paying for use of the lender's money each day until the debt is repaid. That rate is then multiplied by the number of days since your last bill: although that's normally a month, it might vary by a day or two due to holidays and weekends. (In our example in Table 3.2, it's 32 days.) Finally, that monthly rate is multiplied by the amount of money you still owe at that rate.

So in the example above, which rate are you paying? Well . . . a blend of them all. Here's the math to figure it out, but don't worry if it's a bit above your head: the most important interest rate to note is the *highest* one, for reasons we'll get to in a moment. To find the blended rate, follow these steps:

1. Multiply the total owed for each percentage rate by the rate itself. In this case, that's

   $8,460.67 × 14.020 = $118,618.59
   $3,609.18 × 3.990 = $14,400.63
   $1,000.00 × 23.020 = $23,020.00

2. Add up these amounts:

   $118,618.59 + $14,400.63 + $23,020.00 = $156,039.22

3. Add up the original amounts owed:

   $8,460.67 + $3,609.18 + $1,000.00 = $13,069.85

4. Divide the first number by the second:

   $156,039.22 / $13,069.85 = 11.94

You're currently paying an interest rate of 11.94% on this credit card.

However, that interest rate will *increase* as you pay off the debt, until it's at the highest rate listed—in this case, an outrageous 23.02 percent. Why? You might have noticed a blurb on your card agreement that said something like, "We apply your payments to low APR balances first. You cannot pay off higher APR balances until you pay off lower APR balances." Therein lies the rub: any balance you have at a low promotional rate (such as they often give for credit card checks) "locks in" the debt you have at higher rates.

So let's say you suddenly inherit $10,000 and put it all toward this credit card bill. The first $3,609.18 would pay off the amount owed at 3.99 percent, and the remaining $6,390.82 would go toward partially paying off the amount owed at 14.02 percent. The amount owed at 23.02 percent wouldn't be touched at all. And if you went through the math again, you'd find that your effective interest rate after the payment would be 16.95 percent—about a 5 percent increase from before you made the payment. On the other hand, the *amount* you'd owe has gone down substantially, so you would be spending far less per month on interest charges.

Lower Your Credit Card Payments

But let's get back to your credit cards and figure out how we can lower the amount you pay each month on them. There are two ways to lower your payments on a loan:

1. Extend the loan's length, so you pay it off more slowly (but with a lower monthly payment).

2. Pay lower loan costs.

For credit cards, most people take the first route by simply lowering their monthly payment until they're paying only the minimum amount that the card company allows. While that approach solves the immediate problem, in the long run, it's bad policy.

Here's why. The minimum payment amount on a credit card is typically around 2 percent of the total debt. So let's say you bought a home entertainment system and now owe $10,000 on a credit card. Your minimum monthly payment would be about $10,000 × 0.02 = $200. Let's say the card has a 12 percent interest rate, meaning you're paying 1 percent per month just on interest, or $10,000 × 0.01 = $100. So when you pay that minimum of $200, $100 of it goes toward interest, and the other $100 goes toward paying off the $10,000 principal. The next month, you'll owe nearly as much: $10,000 − $100 = $9,900. Your minimum payment will also go down slightly, because it will be calculated as 2 percent of the amount you now owe, or $9,900 × 2% = $198.

You see that bill and say, "Woo-hoo! I only need to pay $198 this month!" and save the two dollars for something else. If you rinse, lather, and repeat every month, guess how long it will take you to pay off the $10,000? Thirty years! And you'll have paid over $9,500 in interest. You'll be paying for those fancy electronics long after they become obsolete.

On the other hand, let's say you commit to paying $200 every month, even as the minimum payment goes down. At that rate, you'll only need six years to pay off the full $10,000 debt and pay just a little under $4,000 in interest. (The online calculator at *www.bankrate.com/brm/calc/MinPayment.asp* can tell you how long you'll need to pay off your credit cards and how much you'll benefit or suffer from changes in payment plans.)

Having been warned against low credit card payments, let's remember Essential Truth #4: Benefits should always outweigh costs. If you determine that those two dollars per month are what's needed to keep you out of foreclosure, do what you must!

Refinance Your Credit Cards (Maybe)

Let's turn to the second route for lowering monthly credit card payments: paying lower loan costs, usually by refinancing the debt through an offer from the same or another credit card company. These offers can be quite tempting, and they can in fact lower your monthly payment. But before you leap, take a moment to review what the loan costs are, how they interact, and how to compare deals to determine whether they'll actually be good for you.

Loan costs are divided into two parts: interest rates and fees. Fees usually happen only once, when you originate the loan. Some recur, however, such as annual credit card membership fees; others appear irregularly, such as late charges. Interest charges, on the other hand, add up every day that you owe money.

Sometimes you'll have to balance fees against interest rates. Is it cheaper to pay an 8 percent rate with no fee or a 6 percent rate with a $100 fee? The answer lies in the amount that you're borrowing and the length of time before you pay it off. You might remember facing a similar question when you first got your mortgage and the broker asked you whether you wanted to pay points, which are a fee paid up front in exchange for a lower interest rate. (We'll discuss points specifically in Chapter 6, "Understand Your Loan.")

To illustrate, we'll start with an extremely simplified example: you borrow $10,000 and will pay it off in full with one payment at the end of a year. As above, you have the choice of taking the loan at an 8 percent interest rate with no fees or a 6 percent interest rate with a $100 fee up front. The better choice, simply put, is the one that takes less of your money. To figure that out, we first have to determine how much interest you'll pay in either case:

- At 8 percent, you'll pay $10,000 × 0.08 = $800 for the year.

- At 6 percent, you'll pay $10,000 × 0.06 = $600 for the year, plus the $100 fee, or a total of $700.

Therefore, the second deal is better, because you'll pay less—$700 for the year rather than $800.

Another way of thinking of such comparisons is to look at the effective APR, which takes fees into account. This is, in fact, how finance professionals compare loans. (We'll examine how effective APRs come to play in your mortgage in Chapter 6, "Understand Your Loan.") In our example here, the effective APR for the loan with 6 percent interest is 7 percent, because $700 / $10,000 = 0.07. To figure out the effective APR of your loan, use the calculator at *www.locallender.info/consumer-banking/mortgage/apr-calculator.asp.* (You'll need to make a guess at how long you'll need to pay off the loan, and the calculator assumes that you'll do it with equal payments every month.)

The next step is to look at ways you could lower those costs. The most direct and cost-effective method is to call the lender or credit card company and ask for a lower rate. Believe it or not, they'll sometimes give it to you! (We'll explain why and walk you through that procedure in Chapter 5, "Call for Help.") But often you'll receive offers from the credit card company and other lenders of a credit-card check or other ways to "consolidate your debt." You might even get such a solicitation from your mortgage company, which ignores the fact that you're nearing foreclosure.

In such deals, the devil is in the details, and in this case, the details are in the small print. These offers are extremely tempting because of the low interest rates they advertise. Certainly 2.9 percent is a lower payment than 12.9 percent, right? The four biggest catches in such offers are these:

1. The advertised rate is valid only for a short time before reverting to a much higher rate. Six months of a 2.9 percent interest rate isn't much consolation if, at the end of the period, the rate jumps to 18.9 percent.

2. The up-front fee is going to cost you. Known by such terms as balance-transfer fee or (if paid using a credit-card check) check fee, the usual amount is 3 percent of the amount borrowed, with no cap (limit). By itself, that's not so bad: if the offer has a nominal APR of 2.9 percent and you pay off the debt in full in one year, that gives you an effective APR of a competitive 5.9 percent. But as we mentioned before, you won't be paying this rate if you have a lot of other debt on the same card at a higher rate. Which leads us to the third big catch . . .

3. These offers "lock in" higher interest rates on the same card. Remember that phrase, "We apply your payments to low APR balances first"? In other words, interest will continue to accrue on the higher-rate portions of your credit card balance until you've paid off the entire promotional loan. To figure out how much you'll actually pay in interest, review the section about blended rates earlier in this chapter.

4. These deals often don't lower your minimum payment. If you're already paying only the minimum each month and your goal is to have more money available to pay your mortgage, such transfers aren't of much help, because your minimum payment is calculated based on total debt, with

no regard to the interest rate or fees. A debt of $10,000 with a 2 percent minimum payment will still require $200 each month, no matter what the interest rate is.

Get Rid of Repeating Expenses

There's a third category of expense eligible for cuts: recurring system-support expenses. In this group, the Lees have only two items: Pat's health insurance and car insurance for both Jo and Pat. Other examples of such expenses would be memberships in professional and recreational groups, monthly costs for recreational properties, storage space, certain utilities, and costs to maintain a hobby. Once again, these are basically just discretionary expenses with one big difference: you can't cut back on them on a day-to-day basis as you can with, say, food or entertainment. Rather, you have to lower or eliminate them in a planned way or not at all.

Because of the all-or-nothing nature of such expenses, they can be especially hard to eliminate. Who wants to admit that they can't afford to pursue a favorite hobby or have an extra car in the family? Further, you might need to make a few phone calls—and even pay penalty fees—to end these expenses. On the flip side, they tend to be large expenses and, therefore, can make a big difference in your monthly budget.

Believe me, I know. For years after graduating with a music degree, I thought of going back to performing. But work and other demands intruded, as they often do. Finally I decided to get serious and, as a token of commitment, joined the local musicians' union at a cost of $250 per year. I remained a member for a few years, cheerfully paying my dues and enjoying jam sessions at the union hall—but I never seriously pursued union work. Finally I came to realize that my membership didn't make me a working musician, even as I carried it as a badge of honor. The $250 per year was a price paid to support my ego and little else, so finally I dropped it.

How many people maintain $600/year gym memberships without ever using the facilities?

Here's a trick to figure out whether memberships are worthwhile. Divide the monthly cost by the number of times you get benefit from the membership. The result is the amount you pay each time you get benefit. For example, say you visit the gym once a week (about four times a month) and your membership costs $50 per month: $50 / 4 visits = $12.50 per visit. Then think to yourself: If I could use this gym on a pay-per-visit basis, would I be willing to take $12.50 in cash out of my pocket every time I walked in the door? If so, fine; if not, consider dropping it.

Using this logic, I sold my car when a change in job no longer required it. I figured that the $500 per month I was paying on the loan and insurance wasn't worth the once-a-week use I got from it. I could certainly rent a car for much less than that $125 per use.

For insurance, it's harder to perform a cost-benefit analysis. After all, in a perfect world, you'd never have to take advantage of the benefits. Fortunately, you can save substantial money by re-examining insurance coverage and cutting it back rather than eliminating it outright. For example, you might have taken out a comprehensive insurance policy on your car when it was new, to reimburse you for loss due to theft, fire, and other problems caused by unknown sources. That might have made sense 10 years ago, when it was worth $20,000, but does it make sense now, when it's only worth a few thousand? Collision insurance is another area where you can easily cut back, although it might mean living with a dented door after a minor accident. As always, weigh the costs and benefits against each other; in any case, a chat with your insurance broker will give you options. If you're truly motivated, you might even want to consider switching insurers: online comparison-shopping sites, such as Insurance.com (*www.insurance.com*), deliver quotes to your computer in minutes.

Recreational properties and storage space are perhaps the hardest expenses to give up, because they're so intimately related to possessions that represent escape, achievement, or warm memories. Ironically, those expenses seem unimportant precisely *because* you don't directly see benefits from them every day. But those benefits come at substantial costs. According to the Self Storage Association (*www.selfstorage.org*), the industry takes in over $22 billion per year in the United States, or about $75 per citizen, renting out space at a rate of about $1 per square foot per month. If you're like many people with a self-storage unit, ask yourself: Do you really need the items in your locker? *Out of sight* might mean out of mind—but in this case it also means out-of-pocket expense. Likewise, consider the summer boat you have docked in a recreational marina or even the broken-down Mustang in the backyard: Are you paying registration and fees for those items? Take a hard look at the benefits you get from them. Then ask yourself whether they're worth more than your ability to pay the mortgage.

Increase Your Income

Saving money is only one way to close the gap between income and expenses. The other, of course, is to make more money. But as mentioned earlier, a penny saved is actually *more* than a penny earned because of taxes. If you're in the 28 percent income tax bracket, every dollar earned equals only $1.00 - $0.28 = $0.72 saved. Put another way, you have to earn about $1.00 / $0.72 = $1.39 to have the benefit of saving a dollar!

But earning more is still a worthwhile pursuit, especially if you've already cut expenses to the bone. Here are some ideas:

- Get a second job, preferably using different skills from those demanded by your "day job" to avoid burnout.

- Sell small, valuable items through eBay or other online auction site.

- Rent space in your home for lodging, parking, or storage.

- Freelance in one of your areas of expertise.

Move Forward

If you've read this far, congratulations! You're now well armed to face consultants, legal professionals, and your creditors with a realistic plan of action. The knowledge and confidence you've gained from understanding your particular situation will stand you in good stead as you discover the options open to you and negotiate for those that best fit your situation. Your mortgage problems underline a financial weakness: I hope that, by getting a handle on your assets, balance sheet, and budget, you have a better sense of your financial strength.

But before you make those phone calls, we have to take a detour down a dark alley to learn about the many ways scammers seek to steal that strength from you for their own gain. In an unfamiliar place, it's hard to tell friends from foes. The next chapter will be your guide.

4

Learn How to
Avoid Scams

Reporter: Why do you rob banks?

Thief: Because that's where the money is.

This colorful response (falsely attributed to bank robber Willie Sutton) explains why far more money is lost to mortgage fraud than bank robbery in the United States: simply put, more wealth is held in real estate than in banks. As you saw in Chapter 2, "Get a Handle on Your Situation," even a homeowner facing foreclosure can have tens or even hundreds of thousands of dollars of wealth in the form of home equity—a tempting target, indeed. And while bank robbery involves a certain amount of physical danger and derring-do, foreclosure scams often involve nothing more than homeowners, heads clouded with desperation, who willingly wield a pen to sign papers they don't understand. Enter a "rescue artist" with a stack of such papers . . . and say goodbye to your home.

You may feel that cloud of despair slipping around you as the weeks go by and you start to wonder how you'll ever get your finances on track again. Who can blame a drowning person for grasping at what looks like a rope—even if it turns out to be a snake? I hope that by learning about common scams and following a few simple guidelines, you'll avoid falling victim to problems much bigger than simply missing a mortgage payment.

But before we go on to horror stories of foreclosure fraud, there are information sources you *can* trust:

- *U.S. Department of Housing and Urban Development (HUD).* HUD hosts a page of resources organized by state (*www. hud.gov/local/*): click on the name of the state where your property is located, then find the "Avoiding Foreclosure" link for resources. Alternately, go directly to *www.hud.gov/local/ xx/homeownership/foreclosure.cfm,* replacing *xx* with your state's two-letter abbreviation. Other resources are at "Tips for Avoiding Foreclosure" (*www.hud.gov/foreclosure/*). HUD also qualifies and approves independent housing counselors in your area and can give you a referral to someone to talk with, one-on-one. As you start to receive strange-seeming solicitations—and you will—this counselor will help you figure out whether they're on the up-and-up.

- *Your lender.* Even if your situation looks hopeless, your lender wants to know about it—and might help you avoid falling prey to scammers. (As you'll see, some scams require that you *not* talk to your existing lender and are easily foiled by making that phone call.) For reasons we'll see in Chapter 5, "Call for Help," the lender really doesn't want your home: foreclosures are far more expensive and troublesome than keeping you in the house. The information you gathered by following the steps in Chapter 2, "Get a Handle on Your

Situation," will help the lender figure out a plan, while the steps you took to fix your budget in Chapter 3, "Rework your Income and Expenses," show that you're willing to meet your lender halfway.

Now prepare yourself for some real ugliness—the dark world of foreclosure scams.

Understand Why People Fall for Foreclosure Scams

In short, most foreclosure scams rely on four factors, working together. The good news is that you can defeat them by removing any of these factors, each of which take aim at understandable, human vulnerabilities.

1. *Homeowners who don't know the value of their homes' equity or how to turn it into money.* Remember our friends, the Lees? You might remember from their list of assets and liabilities (Table 2.2) that they calculated the market value of their home at $430,000 yet only owed a little over $335,000 on it (as mortgages of $278,378 and $57,000). That means they have gross equity of $430,000 − $335,000 = $95,000 in their home. They could turn that equity into cash in several ways—we'll describe some of them in Chapter 6, "Understand Your Loan."

   Scammers, relying on the fact that many homeowners aren't knowledgeable about these techniques, are able to buy that $95,000 of value for a very, very low price. Sometimes they use arrangements that are deliberately complicated to hide their machinations, but the end result is the same: you trade a nugget of gold for a sliver of silver.

2. *Willingness to sign papers without reading or understanding them fully.* During the housing boom, I did some work as a "notary signing agent"—that is, someone who sits with sellers, buyers, and borrowers at closing to certify their identities and show them where to sign. Professionals who usually performed that function—such as escrow officers in my own state of California—were simply too busy to do what they saw as a purely clerical function. Those who did oversee closings were often rushed for time and encouraged everybody to sign quickly—even though the parties usually had never seen the paperwork before! Further, both escrow officers and notary signing agents are forbidden from explaining the papers in much detail, because that could be considered "practicing law," an act that requires an attorney's license.

Sadly, the vast majority of people are willing to sign such crucial papers without completely understanding their contents. That's usually not a problem because most deals are honest, but scammers easily take advantage of this tendency to include terms that differ outrageously from verbal agreements. And as they say, in a court of law, a verbal agreement "is worth the paper it's written on"—that is, nothing. If you don't understand and agree with the written terms of a contract, don't sign it, even if that means the bank will sell off your home the next day.

3. *Susceptibility to behavior-control tricks and high-pressure sales techniques.* Movies have done us a great disservice by depicting villains as devious-looking, shifty-eyed cartoons. In reality, they're more likely to look like a beloved uncle or a slightly bumbling friend. You might even feel pity for them as they blush over "mistakes"—but if the deal's bad, none of that matters. Deal with the offer, not the person; ignore threats, flirtation, jokes, and other distractions that

prevent you from asking questions and getting answers. And don't be afraid to be rude! It's better to offend someone than to lose your life's savings because you were too shy to speak up. The written contract is what matters, not the person who hands it to you.

4. *Desperation to try anything to keep one's home, sometimes coupled with good old-fashioned greed and wishful thinking.* One common theme in underhanded foreclosure schemes is that you *need* to sign. It's the only way to avoid foreclosure, they say, or the alternatives are much worse. Sometimes the scammer will sweeten the pot by throwing in some actual cash, perhaps to pay off other debts (such as credit cards). You're in hell, and the scammer offers you a shot at heaven: How could you possibly say no?

Breaking the illusion takes two steps. First, remember Essential Truth #2: There is no magic bullet. If one "solution" seems to avoid the pitfalls of all others, you can bet you're not getting the full story. When in hell, shoot for earth, not heaven. Second, consider Essential Truth #3: You have options. Don't let anyone tell you differently.

Learn the Three Most Common Scams

The nonprofit National Consumer Law Center (NCLC) identifies three main forms of foreclosure scam in its 2005 report "Dreams Foreclosed," which is free on its website, *www.consumerlaw.org*.

Phantom Help

The first scam it calls "phantom help." A foreclosure "counselor" or "expert" promises to intervene on your behalf by filing papers and undertaking negotiations with lenders that (they say) are too obscure or difficult for you to do yourself. And, in fact, they may do exactly as they say—for a fee. But you don't need anyone to represent you when you talk with your lender. In fact, you're better off making the connection yourself, because the lender believes that *you* know your situation best and will ultimately be responsible for any deal the two of you work out.

At the very least, you'll pay for services you could get for free from a HUD-approved housing counseling agency; at worst, the scammer will promise impossible things, such as getting the lender to forgive your debt. Then, after getting hundreds or even thousands of dollars from you in fees, the con artist will disappear or make some excuse as to why you didn't get the help you expected. The real reason is clear: the scammer never had any powers that you don't have yourself! (The NCLC report includes copies of some contracts used by such companies, and among their clauses, sprinkled amid the small print, is "no . . . outcome guarantee is made or implied.")

The Bailout

The second variety of scam, which the report calls "the 'bailout' that never quite works," requires you to sign your home over to the scammer. This might be hard to believe, but the story the con artist tells sounds so good and homeowners are often so desperate, many fall for it. Here's a typical tale. Let's say you owe $250,000 on a home worth $300,000. The "rescue artists" tell you to sign over the deed, sometimes calling it a sale/leaseback deal. They'll make all the payments, they say, and you can rent your home from them until you get back on your feet again, at which point (they say) they'll sell it back to you. Sometimes they'll even throw in a few thousand dollars or pay off other debts. It sounds good, doesn't it? If it worked the way they say, you'd pay rent that's much more affordable than the mortgage, get out of foreclosure, and get your home back when the troubles pass.

The problem is this: it's no longer your home, and you're never getting it back. Once they have the deed, they can do pretty much whatever they want, with no intention of ever giving your house back to you. Usually they won't even make payments on the mortgage—why should they? Instead, they start a process called equity stripping, where they convert that $50,000 into cash that goes straight into their pockets. Maybe they take out a loan for that amount, or they may find a way to claim it in "fees" when you sign all the paperwork. In any case, they then skip town and let the bank foreclose on the mortgage. Meanwhile (depending on how the deal was arranged), you've lost all the equity you've built up, are getting evicted from your home, might still be on the hook for the full value of the loan . . . and have been paying rent to the scammers as well!

Paper Shuffling

The third kind of scam described by the report is a simple paper shuffling, whereby the fraudsters make up a story about how the papers you're signing will solve your foreclosure problem. In fact, signing those papers grants them powers to refinance your home (to their advantage) or deed it to them entirely. Again, the solution is simple: don't sign papers you don't understand and agree with!

Other Schemes

Widely found "in the wild" (but not described by the NCLC report) are schemes whereby a scammer convinces you to falsify documents or enter into complicated financing arrangements intended to defraud the lender. (Finance professor and writer Jack Guttentag lists many of these on his website at *www. mtgprofessor.com/scams.htm.*) A common scam has you get an appraisal for your property that's well above its actual value and take out a loan based on that value. In return, the scammer either takes a cut or collects some large "brokerage" fees. You end up attempting to pay off a larger loan than before and could be liable for fraud charges yourself when the lender finds out. Foreclosure is bad enough: jail is worse!

Finally, there's a much more mundane form of scam, where mortgage brokers steer you into a series of loans that don't make much sense but that result in more and more fees going into their pockets. This is a slow form of equity stripping, as often the brokers arrange it so you don't pay their fees directly. Instead, the fees are simply added to the loan amount. The lender pays the dishonest broker, you owe an extra $10,000 (or $20,000 or $50,000), the broker promises that yet another refinance will solve the problem . . . and eventually the house of cards falls down.

All these schemes share one characteristic: they transfer money or property to someone in an amount far beyond normal fees for the services provided. If the scammers simply demanded that you take the money out of your pocket, you'd see them for the muggers they are. Instead, they take money from you bit by bit, fool you into financing the cost over time, or trick you into helping them steal it from the lender. In the harshest form of foreclosure fraud, you could actually lose your home itself.

Stay Open to Good, Legitimate Deals

At this point you might be thinking, "Everyone involved in foreclosure management is a thief!" And indeed, scams look very much like legitimate solutions. That's by design, of course: con artists go to great lengths to copy the language and appearance of legitimate business practices precisely so the unknowing will naturally confuse the two. They have nice-looking websites, stationery, printed forms, suits, and sometimes even offices—just like their legitimate next-door neighbors. Often they have names intended to disguise their actual business or that can easily be confused with a trusted, better-known source.

But take heart: some plans are not only legitimate but potentially of genuine help—as long as the terms are fair. Here are a few:

- *Some types of refinancing.* One of the most popular ways to get out of foreclosure is simply to get a new loan and pay off the old one. Unfortunately, "tricky" refinances are also one of the most popular scams. We'll talk about how to tell which are fair and beneficial in Chapter 6, "Understand Your Loan." In brief, a new loan should be sustainable in the long run, be based on a fair valuation of the home, have clear and unambiguous terms, carry fees and charges in the range of similar loans, and (ideally) maintain your equity. And, of course, it should require a lower monthly payment from you. (If it doesn't, what's the point?)

- *Selling your home for a fair value.* When I started writing this book, about 30 out of 35 books on the market with *foreclosure* in their titles taught readers how to get rich by *buying* foreclosed properties from homeowners in trouble. I can save you the cost of those 30 books by giving you their secret: buy low, sell high. That's it! Profits are based on the idea that you can buy properties "in distress" for less than their market value, then resell them at the market rate and pocket the difference. As the prospective seller, then, you should be aware that most "buy my home" offers you get are going to be well below the price you'd get by advertising your home on the open market.

In some cases, it might make sense to sell your home for below market value, such as when you need the money sooner than the traditional sales process could offer, if you'd save transaction costs that are larger than the difference in price, or in exchange for some other valuable consideration. But those situations are the exception to the rule. If you must sell, why not get as much as you can? You'll see how to do that in Chapter 8, "Sell Before the Pain Starts."

■ *Selling certain rights to your home.* Real estate professionals refer to property ownership as a bundle of rights, because it's somewhat more complicated than owning, say, a bicycle. For example, you might own your home but not have the right to prevent your neighbors from walking across your front lawn, if they have an easement that allows them to do that. With that in mind, you might be able to squeeze money from your home by selling "sticks" from this bundle. Is that a good idea? As always, it depends on the terms: What will you lose? And what you gain?

A simple example would be if you rented out a bedroom. In essence, you would be selling the right to occupy that room for a limited time in exchange for the rent money. Or you might sell the rights to collect apples from an orchard on your property. A more complicated (and serious) example would be sale of a remainderman position, whereby you would be permitted to live in the property until your death and it would be transferred to someone else at that point. Yet another is when someone becomes an equity partner who pays you for a percentage share in your home with the expectation that they'll make money from its appreciation when you sell.

Such deals are fairly uncommon, so we won't discuss them in great detail. As with any offer, remember Essential Truth #4: Benefits should always outweigh costs. If they don't, or you don't fully understand either side of the equation, pass it by.

Beware These Red Flags

So how can you tell scams from the real deal? Here are some red flags that should cause you to be suspicious of a proposed "solution":

- *It's advertised through illegal means.* A wide variety of illegal advertising means exist, bedeviling property owners and the public at large. Especially visible in the mortgage and real estate fields are signs posted on public or private property, for example next to a highway off-ramp, without permission or proper licenses. Such signs are called "bandit signs" or "snipe signs" and are particularly common among real estate investors who claim to "Buy any home!" for cash. Also frequently seen are emails and faxes advertising mortgage offers from people you don't know. These are generally also illegal. Even in the few cases where such advertising isn't *technically* illegal, the cost of the message is stolen from the person who receives or hosts it, not the person who sends it. Such a company starts out by ripping you off before you even engage their services; that's not a company you can trust!

Professor Guttentag has written that you should be suspicious of *all* "rescue" advertising, saying, "While not all those who solicit are rogues, all rogues solicit, which means the odds are against you when you respond." I don't dislike advertised services as he appears to, but his point is well taken.

A side note: Be wary of any foreclosure-rescue website that has a link offering to let you become an "affiliate," which is a fancy word for salesperson. That's a sign of a kind of marketing that's found only on commercial, for-profit sites. Money paid to "affiliates" comes straight from the pockets of the people such companies are supposed to help—in other words, you. Also, don't be fooled by small graphic badges that claim membership in the Better Business Bureau or any other organization: the vast majority are "pay for play" honors, not a true sign of legitimacy.

■ *You're required to pay money up front without receiving a clear benefit.* This requirement is most common among the phantom help scammers, where you're supposed to pay for "counseling" or something similar. But plenty of agencies offer the same services without cost. As the nonprofit Homeownership Preservation Foundation (*www.995hope.org*) says, "Foreclosure advice and direction should always be free."

Two fees you might legitimately have to pay up front are to order a credit report (typically about $20) or have the property appraised (a few hundred bucks) in the process of refinancing. In both cases, the money goes to a third party—the credit-reporting agency or appraiser—*not* the counselor or mortgage broker. Other fees might be common and legitimate in your region: ask a real estate professional if you're unsure.

■ *You're told to sign papers that have blank spaces or false information.* When you sign your name, you're saying "I agree with (or at least acknowledge) everything on this document." How could you possibly agree with information that's not there yet or that you know to be untrue?

■ *You're pressured to act without the opportunity to talk to outside counsel or your existing lender and without time to read and understand the paperwork fully.* Fear, isolation, doubt, confusion, hurry . . . these all undermine your ability to make clear decisions. They are your enemies and the friends of those who are trying to trick you. A saying from the restaurant industry is just as true here: "When in doubt, throw it out."

■ *The deal requires hiding information.* Quite a few mortgage scams involve giving different stories to two parties. For example, you're supposed to tell Lender #1 that you're not getting any other loans on the property, even though Lender #2 knows otherwise. This lying by omission and is just as bad—and legally actionable—as the more-familiar form of lying by commission. Further, keep in mind the popular saying that "there is no honor among thieves." If they're telling you to hide something from others, what are they hiding from you?

■ *Your benefits depend on an unwritten promise.* "You can refinance at a much better rate in a month." "We'll refund all your costs." "You'll buy your property back from us at a discount after the money comes in." These are all just promises scammers give homeowners to get them to sign on the dotted line, with no intention of following through. There's a saying in legal circles: "A contract lives within the document's four corners." While sometimes judges will consider outside influences (such as whether it was signed under duress), the written contract comes first. If the offerors won't put it in writing, they're either afraid of something being discovered (see above) or they don't intend to honor their promises at all.

- *You're required to change how the property's held (its vesting).* One scam involves putting your home into a newly created trust, typically with a name that implies it still belongs to you (e.g., The Jo and Pat Lee 123 Home Street Trust), but with the scammer as the trustee. Trusts are in fact largely controlled by the trustee, and from there, it's an easy matter to wrest the last semblances of ownership from your hands.

- *You don't completely understand the details.* As comedian W. C. Fields said, "If you can't dazzle them with brilliance, baffle them with bull." Many scams are unnecessarily complicated to prevent you from being able to make apples-to-apples comparisons of costs and benefits. If you don't understand it, walk away.

Move Forward

Much of life is preparation, and up until now you've been readying yourself and your files to face the music. But saving your home can't be done any other way. Just as the gymnast stretches and exercises for years to perform a three-second vault, so has your education and information gathering made possible some challenging communications with lenders, attorneys, and real estate professionals. Now it's time to take to the mat, but don't worry: your hard work is about to pay off. Forward!

Call for Help

Most foreclosure advisors, after learning your name and shaking your hand, start with the same three words: "Call your lender." They know that that's usually the number one thing that people facing foreclosure are most afraid to do—and the fastest way to resolve problems. Some scared homeowners believe that lenders will jump on any sign of weakness to wrest their home away, change their loan terms, ruin their credit, or somehow otherwise take advantage of them—all on the basis of one phone call.

Embarrassment and shame also prevent people from telling others about their financial woes, even when doing so will end those problems. As visitors from outside the United States often observe, money is a touchy subject for most Americans. On one hand, we're not shy about asking how much something costs—a practice many outside the country find crass. On the other, much of our self-esteem is tied up in earnings, possessions, and financial security. As writer Kurt Vonnegut Jr. pointed out in *Slaughterhouse Five,* "It ain't no disgrace to be poor, but it might as well be."

There are three problems with starting foreclosure advice with "call your lender." First, you'll need certain information in hand when you call lenders and others. We got ahead of the game by collecting that information in Chapter 2, "Get a Handle on Your Situation." Second, you can often get out of trouble with a simple rebudgeting, as we did in Chapter 3, "Rework Your Income and Expenses." Finally, many homeowners get waylaid by the temptation of bad deals before they have a chance to reach out. We also led you through that valley of thieves in Chapter 4, "Learn How to Avoid Scams."

Now it's time to make some phone calls.

Call Your Lender

Your first phone call will be to the loss-mitigation department of your lender—that is, the lender who holds the mortgage you're having trouble paying. *Mitigation* means "reduction." In other words, the lender sees your foreclosure as a *loss* to the financial institution as well as to you, and wants to make it as small as possible. That's quite different from the force-'em-into-foreclosure-and-grab-their-house fantasy described above! In reality, foreclosures are just as bad for the lender as they are for you. Lenders have two options:

1. Go through a lot of paperwork, and possibly the legal system, to get you out of your home. Have several uncomfortable confrontations with you while enduring the heartbreak of your situation. (Remember, there are people on the other end of the phones: they have hearts too.) Possibly renovate or clean parts of the home to make it saleable. Continue paying holding costs (for taxes,

maintenance, etc.) for weeks, months, or even years while searching for a buyer. Pay real estate professionals to sell the home, process the escrow . . .

2. Let you stay in your home while you delay or skip a few payments, maybe with a change in loan terms.

Seen this way, it's easy to understand why lenders are loath to let your property go into foreclosure! According to a study by financial research company TowerGroup, lenders lose an average of about *$59,000* per foreclosure. Lenders know that foreclosures are going to happen, of course: they just want them to be as cheap as possible.

But whom should you contact? In the simplest of cases, it's the company that gave you the loan in the first place, whether that's the purchase-money lender or a lender who later helped you refinance. But loans often get traded from lender to lender, so there's a good chance that the company you contact will have an unfamiliar name. If so, you should have received a document when your loan changed hands. Actually, you should start receiving special communications from your lender about the possibility of foreclosure, starting about a month after you first miss a payment, in the form of a borrower information packet that explains how to avoid foreclosure. The main reason you might not receive that is if the lender doesn't have your correct address. If that's the case, the burden of contact is on you. You might have to do some detective work, but any paperwork you have regarding your loan will give you a place to start. If all else fails, you might be able to get some help from a friendly mortgage broker, escrow officer, or real estate attorney, all of whom have access to professional resources.

You might also find that the phone number on your paperwork leads to a loan servicer rather than the lender itself. In fact, you might not ever find out the actual name of the lender. That's okay. In any case, you're only bound by the terms of the original loan agreement, no matter how many times the loan has changed hands, whether the current lender uses a loan servicer, or the condition of any of the companies involved. (Every once in a while, a rumor surfaces that you don't have to pay your loans if the lender goes out of business. Don't believe it, because it's not true.)

Typically, the person on the other end of the phone deals with difficult situations like yours all day. You see your mortgage in terms of the comfort your home's given you, the future you planned, and the despair caused by the prospect of losing it; on the other end, it's seen in terms of payoffs and probabilities.

That person's questions will reflect those priorities. How soon can you pay? How much? Will you be able to pay if we change the loan terms? In what way? And so forth. If your problems are temporary and you have a good borrowing history, they might be able to find a workout—that is, a solution—right then and there. But don't count on it. That first phone call is really just to get the conversation started and to determine what's possible.

The lender keeps a file about your loan on computer, and notes from this conversation will go into it. Some lenders (and servicers) try to assign the same loss-mitigation person to a file throughout the workout period, which is nice: it never hurts to be on a first-name basis with someone who comes to know your particular situation. But some larger lenders don't do things that way, and at any lender, people quit or take vacations. So don't feel bad if you find yourself passed among members of a loss-mitigation team. If they're on the ball, the file they keep on you will hold information that allows anyone to pick up where the last person left off.

Renegotiate Your Loan

How will the lender respond? Well, it's not just going to forgive the debt! But it *can* do several things as part of a workout plan.

Payment Deferral

You could ask the lender for permission to defer payments for a while. Sometimes, a foreclosure problem is caused by bad planning, and nothing short of a radically higher income will fix it. But at least as often, the problem is due to temporary issues. In our example, the Lees are facing the double whammy of medical problems and lower-than-expected income. While difficult, both of these are likely to be temporary. If the lender believes that your issues will pass, it might allow you to defer payments. A deferment essentially says, "Stop giving us money for a while. You'll start paying again in a few months when these problems have passed, and we'll go from there."

That doesn't mean that any part of the debt is forgiven! In fact, a deferment ultimately puts a lot *more* of your money in the lender's pocket, because you're charged interest on the full amount you owe. That unpaid interest gets added to the principal, increasing your indebtedness.

Let's try an example. Say your mortgage is currently $2,000 per month, with an outstanding balance of $200,000. You have a 6 percent interest rate; that is, 0.5 percent per month. At that interest rate, you're paying $200,000 × 0.005 = $1,000 per month in interest, with $1,000 going toward the principal. If you take a six-month deferment, the $1,000 you owe in interest will be added to the principal each month, so you'll end the first month owing $201,000. You now owe interest of 0.05 percent on that extra $1,000 ($5) in addition to the interest on the original principal, so you end the second month owing $201,000 + $1,000 + $5 = $202,005. This progression is shown in Table 5.1.

When the six months are up, you'll owe, not the original $200,000, but over $206,000! Further, you won't have been paying down the principal, so you'll be over $12,000 further in the hole than if you'd been able to pay your mortgage all along.

The other thing to watch out for with deferments: It can be psychologically difficult to start paying again when the deferment is over. A common response to getting a deferment plan is giddiness. You might think, "We've been saved! Let's take it easy for a while because we don't need to pay the mortgage this month!" In reality, you have to work twice as hard to be sure that you'll be ready when the deferment is over. For one thing, a deferment ruins your habit of paying every month, and habits are hard to pick up again. But more importantly, your lender is unlikely to give you a second chance if you mess up with this one. A deferment is a temporary reprieve, not a pardon.

One strategy I recommend is to accept a deferment but put as much money as possible into a savings account each month

Table 5.1. *Sample Mortgage Deferment*

If you pay every month:

Month	Total Owed	Payment Made	Interest Portion Paid	Principal Portion Paid
Start	$200,000	$2,000	$1,000.00	$1,000.00
1	$199,000	$2,000	$995.00	$1,005.00
2	$197,995	$2,000	$989.98	$1,010.03
3	$196,985	$2,000	$984.92	$1,015.08
4	$195,970	$2,000	$979.85	$1,020.15
5	$194,950	$2,000	$974.75	$1,025.25
6	$193,924	$2,000	$969.62	$1,030.38

If you defer for six months:

Month	Total Owed	Payment Made	Interest (Added to the Principal)
Start	$200,000	$0	$1,000.00
1	$201,000	$0	$1,005.00
2	$202,005	$0	$1,010.03
3	$203,015	$0	$1,015.08
4	$204,030	$0	$1,020.15
5	$205,050	$0	$1,025.25
6	$206,076	$0	$1,030.38

the mortgage is deferred. Let's say, for example, your mortgage payments are $2,000 per month when you lose your job. Your partner's income lets you still pay $1,000 per month toward housing, clearly not enough to come close to the usual mortgage payment, but still something. There's no point in struggling to make impossible payments for the four months you think it'll take you to get another job and start getting paychecks again. Instead, get a deferment for four months (or more) but save that monthly $1,000. If your job search takes longer than expected, you'll be able to pay for two "extra" months of mortgage with the $4,000 you socked away.

Payment Plan Modification

Your lender could offer to modify your payment plan. A payment modification is very much like a deferment. But instead of waiving payments entirely, the lender allows you to reduce them or make some other arrangement that fits your situation. That might mean a flat reduction for a period of time—from $2,000 to $1,500, say—or it could be some sort of variable payment plan. One popular modification is to change an amortizing loan—that is, one where you pay off part of the principal in addition to interest—to an interest-only loan. In any case, don't agree to a payment plan that you don't believe you can truly fulfill: the lender won't be as patient with you a second time if you mess up.

As with a deferment, you're still liable for interest costs on the full amount you owe. If you're paying an amount less than the interest, you'll end the workout period owing more than when you started.

Loan Terms Modification

You could ask to modify your loan terms. Two things happen as a loan ages: the end date approaches, and you pay off more and more of the principal with each payment (assuming that it's not an interest-only loan). Both of these factors allow a certain amount of flexibility in your loan that the lender can work with.

Extending your loan's end date (or termination date) is a simple procedure and can make an enormous difference in your monthly payment. For example, let's pretend you have a $100,000, 30-year mortgage that began 5 years (60 months) ago at a fixed 6.5 percent interest rate. The monthly payment would be about $632. Now you're having a hard time meeting the monthly payment, and the lender suggests extending the loan term from the current 25 years (30 years minus the 5 years already passed) to a full 30 years again. The principal has gone down to about $93,600, and financing that amount with a 30-year loan lowers your monthly payment to $592—a savings of about $40 per month.

Maybe that's not very impressive savings, but the discount goes up substantially the longer you've held your loan before extending it. That's because of how amortized loans work, which we'll explain in Chapter 6, "Understand your Loan." Table 5.2 shows an example.

The downside is obvious: you'll be paying off your loan for longer than you would be otherwise—possibly much, much longer.

As another benefit, however, your original loan may have become less advantageous than currently available loans if interest rates have fallen or new loan products have become available. If, for example, you took out a fixed-rate loan with an 8 percent interest rate and the same loan is now available at a 7 percent interest rate, you could save hundreds of dollars every month by making

Table 5.2. *Effects of Loan Extension*

Amount you'd pay every month if you extended a $100,000 loan at 6.5 percent to 30 years:

Years Held Before Extending	Principal Amount	Monthly Payment	Monthly Savings
0	$100,000	$632	$0
5	$93,611	$592	$40
10	$84,776	$536	$96
15	$72,559	$459	$173
20	$55,664	$352	$280
25	$32,303	$204	$428

the switch. These other loan options could tempt you to switch lenders, and your current lender doesn't want to lose your business! Therefore, it might agree to modify your loan to 7 percent to ensure that your money continues to go into its pockets.

Refinance with a New Loan

The lender might offer to refinance with a new loan. Sometimes borrowers find themselves in a loan that simply doesn't make any sense. One example would be a couple who bought their home with the expectation that they would be there the rest of their lives, so they took out a 30-year, fixed-rate loan. Then they discovered that the company where they work is planning to move to another city in five years. They love their jobs and want to be ready to move when the time comes. They would be a good candidate for a shorter-term loan, possibly with a variable rate. Such loans usually have a much lower interest rate, which would save them money from month to month. And they don't care that the rate is going to increase substantially at the end of five years, because they intend to sell their home before that happens.

Most of the foreclosure "solutions" you see advertised on the Internet are by mortgage brokers trying to convince you to lower your monthly payment by moving into a variable-rate loan with a low initial teaser rate. (We'll discuss such loans in greater detail in Chapter 6, "Understand Your Loan.") And sure enough, your monthly payment *will* be lower—at least, at first.

In fact, your monthly payments might be lower even if you refinance into a higher-rate loan. How is this possible? Every time you refinance, it "restarts the clock," so to speak, as new loans are almost all figured on a 30-year amortization schedule. As a result, refinancing gives you a benefit similar to that of extending the loan term with your original lender, as was described above.

However, refinancing has additional costs in the form of loan fees—fees that go straight into the mortgage broker's pocket. You probably won't have to pay these fees up front, as they're simply added to your principal and financed over the life of the loan. But pay them you will, over 30 years.

By way of example, let's take our earlier loan of $100,000 with fixed-rate 6.5 percent interest that was originated five years ago and has a $632 monthly payment. As mentioned, you've paid down the principal to about $93,600, so refinancing with a new loan under the same terms would require only a $592 payment per month. So far, so good. But what if the loan fees were

$3,000? Then the principal you'd need to finance goes back up to $93,600 + $3,000 = $97,600, bringing your monthly payment back up to $617 per month. In other words, you'd lose nearly five years of payment history, totaling $632 × 60 = $37,920 to save $15 per month!

Is it worth it? Well . . . sometimes. As always, apply Essential Truth #4: Benefits should always outweigh costs. If that $15 per month allows you to keep your home, then by all means it's worth it. On the other hand, you saw techniques in Chapter 3, "Rework Your Income and Expenses," that could allow you to save at least as much as a refinance would—without costing you tens of thousands of dollars.

Having said that, at times a refinance makes sense even if it doesn't lower your monthly payment. Many people who bought with adjustable-rate mortgages five years ago—like our fictional family, the Lees—are happy to pay thousands of dollars in fees to escape rate increases by moving to a fixed-rate loan. But beware the mortgage broker who pushes refinance after refinance, as some scammers do: they're hunting for fees, not the best deal for you.

Explore Other Solutions

Reinstatement

If you think you'll be able to get caught up soon, you could ask your lender for a reinstatement, wherein you pay everything you owe until the current date, plus outstanding fees and costs, in one big lump sum in return for resuming the loan as before. You might think, "if I could do that, I wouldn't be facing foreclosure in the first place!" But reinstatement has important benefits.

First of all, reinstatement settles your account. You no longer have to dodge phone calls or lose sleep wondering how long you can go without paying before the lender forecloses. You avoid derogatory notes on your credit report that could cause you problems when you try to get other forms of credit, such as a loan on your next home or a refinance on your current home. And you've shown your lenders that you're acting in good faith, so they're more likely to give you a break.

Secondly, a reinstatement plan delays the process while you work out a way to make the lump-sum payment. The lenders know that you don't have ready cash: if you did, you'd have paid your mortgage all along as planned. But they also know that even people who can't pay their mortgage often have hidden resources they could tap for a single, large loan. If you can show them how you'll get caught up in a few months, they're likely to wait.

Thirdly, sometimes the lender requires reinstatement as a condition for working out some other solution, such as a modification of loan terms or deferment of payments.

So where are you going to get the money for reinstatement? Here are some ideas: loans from family members; sale of physical assets such as vehicles and valuables; sale of stocks, bonds, or other securities; and even credit cards. As always, consider the costs of securing this money and weigh them against the benefit of making nice with the lender.

Full Escape

If all else fails, you could propose a full escape. After considering your case, the lender might simply shake its collective head and tell you that it doesn't see any way to help you keep your home. We'll discuss ways to sell your home in a controlled and profitable way in Chapter 8, "Sell Before the Pain Starts," but there is one thing the lender can do to save you the trouble: offer to buy your home for the outstanding value of the loan. Such a deal is called a deed in lieu of foreclosure, or simply a deed in lieu (DIL).

Why would a lender do that? Well, as we mentioned before, lenders hate the foreclosure process as much as you do, both for the trouble and the expense—in addition to the bad feeling it can generate in the community. Like you, they'll do a cost-benefit analysis to determine the value of the deed versus the cost of the foreclosure and follow the most profitable path.

A deed in lieu is most profitable for the lender when the loan amount is low and the value of the property is high; it's most profitable for you when the opposite is true. You have one advantage: lenders' practices are scrutinized by government agencies to prevent them from taking advantage of less-sophisticated property owners. (To get a sense of the mind-spinning regulations lenders have to follow in relation to foreclosure, take a look at HUD's "Loss Mitigation Policy & Guidance" page at *www.hud.gov/offices/hsg/sfh/nsc/lmmltrs.cfm*.) Out of fear that they'll be seen as predatory, therefore, lenders are unlikely to offer a deed in lieu when the loan value is much lower than the home's fair market value. In short, they won't get your $300,000 home for $100,000. Instead, they're likely to offer one of the other workout plans or suggest you sell your home. Amazingly, you're more likely to be able to negotiate a deed in lieu if your $300,000 home has $350,000 in loans on it!

There is a downside, of course. If the home is worth less than the loan amount—$50,000 less, in our example above—the difference could be taxed as income by the Internal Revenue Service. (The December passage of The Mortgage Forgiveness Debt Relief Act of 2007 (H.R. 3648) exempts most homeowners from this tax.) Also, giving your deed in lieu of foreclosure could affect your credit rating and have other financial implications. These issues are beyond the scope of this book: talk with a qualified accountant, attorney, or tax specialist for details on how such a workout would affect your specific situation.

The lender might say that your situation requires you to lose the house but that it's not willing to take a deed in lieu. If so, you might find you can't sell your home for as much as you owe, in which case you'll have to ask the lender whether it will accept a short sale—that is, sale proceeds that are lower than the loan amount. For example, let's say you have $180,000 owing on a home you believe is worth $220,000. But the best offer you receive is $190,000, and the cost of sale is $15,000, leaving you with only $175,000 to pay off that $180,000 debt. The lender might decide that's close enough and permit the short sale; if it doesn't, you'll have to either take the $55,000 loss, let the property go to the foreclosure, or work out another solution.

Here's where that mortgage estoppel letter (or payoff demand) that we mentioned earlier comes in handy. You need to know exactly how much money the lender needs to be satisfied—and, if you come in short, how far off you are. The letter affirms the exact amount you owe including fees, and is necessary for negotiating a short sale.

Eliminate Unneeded Mortgage Insurance

There is one other way you can cut down on the monthly cost of your loan. Your lender probably won't suggest it, and it's only available to homeowners who owe less than 80 percent of the home's current value: ask to get rid of mortgage insurance (MI), if you have any. We'll describe MI in Chapter 6, "Understand Your Loan," but basically it's an additional monthly charge your lender may require when your loan is greater than 80 percent of the home's value.

The lender is supposed to drop the monthly MI charge automatically when your loan falls below 78 percent of your home's original purchase price—for example, $156,000 on a $200,000 home. However, you can request that the lender drop it when appreciation causes your home's value to rise so that the loan is below 80 percent of its *current* market value.

So let's say you bought that $200,000 home with a 95 percent ($190,000) loan. You now owe $185,000 on the loan but believe that your home's gone up in value substantially. How much would it have to increase such that $185,000 is 80 percent of the new value? Simple division tells us: current loan amount / 80% = $185,000 / 0.8 = $231,250. A visit to the automated valuation model websites mentioned in Chapter 2, "Get a Handle on Your Situation," such as Zillow or Cyberhomes, tells you that your home is now worth somewhere around $250,000. You're in business!

If your home's not quite there yet, the calculator at the Mortgage Professor's website (*www.mtgprofessor.com/mpcalculators/Mortgage InsuranceTermination/MtgInsTerminate.asp*) will help you determine when you're likely to be able to remove mortgage insurance, based on your guess at future appreciation rates.

How much will you save? Private mortgage insurance typically costs 0.25 to 1 percent annually on the original loan amount, so for the $190,000 loan above, savings would likely be somewhere between $40 and $160 per month.

Other forms of mortgage insurance are offered by the U.S. Department of Veterans Affairs (VA) and the Federal Housing Administration (FHA); these have their own termination rules, for which you'll need to contact those agencies. We'll give a bit more detail on them in Chapter 7, "Take Advantage of Government Programs."

Contact Others Who Can Help

Besides your lender, there are other places you can call for help.

Other lenders. We mentioned above that your bank might offer to refinance your property, and heaven knows you'll get pitches from J. Random Mortgage Broker. But you don't just have to sit there and wait for a lender on a white steed to ride along and save you. You can find your own loan. In fact, I would recommend you talk with several other lenders no matter what: the most convenient deal isn't always the best one!

Maybe you felt the mortgage brokers you used when you bought your home treated you well. By all means, contact them again. In addition, it's a good idea to get a few competitive quotes. Mortgage brokers expect that you'll comparison shop and are set up to respond quickly to your refinance requests. Several websites—such as *www.bankrate.com, www.lendingtree.com,* and *www.eloan.com*—offer a way to solicit quotes from several lenders at once by entering your details into a single form.

In any case you'll need to have all your information handy, including your current mortgage balance (or balances), terms of current loans, details on your financial capability, and so forth. To compare the resulting offers, see Chapter 6, "Understand Your Loan," for guidelines.

Nonprofit counselors. Remember the "phantom help" scams we described in Chapter 4, "Learn How to Avoid Scams"? You might recall that numerous foreclosure experts will promise assistance—for a fee. But you don't need to pay any such fee, as dozens of nonprofit organizations are set up to provide the same services for free. The U.S. Department of Housing and Urban Development's list at *www.hud.gov/local/* and other resources listed in Chapter 7, "Take Advantage of Government Programs," will lead you to one near you. If there's a possibility you'll file for bankruptcy, try to find a counselor who's also on the Department of Justice's list at *www.usdoj.gov/ust/eo/bapcpa/ccde.*

So what can you expect from such an agency? First and foremost, it exists to provide advice, most of which echoes what's in this book. If you had trouble gathering your paperwork in Chapter 2, "Get a Handle on Your Situation," because of a difficult-to-contact lender or the like, it might have resources that will break through the wall. Some agencies will actually help you contact and speak with the lenders. That's helpful for two reasons: they know lenders' vocabulary and practices, and they're able to speak more dispassionately because they're not personally involved in the outcome. On the other hand, you always run an increased risk of miscommunication when speaking through a representative, and you lose a certain amount of control. Personally, I prefer to do as much negotiation as possible myself, but you should do whatever's most comfortable and effective for you.

A private attorney. There's a good chance that your counselors at some point will tell you that your particular issues are beyond what they're qualified to handle and that you'll have to consult an attorney. Your local Bar Association can help you find one that you can afford: see the directory at *www.abanet.org/legalservices/findlegalhelp/home.cfm* and ask the local chapter about its referral service. *Definitely* contact an attorney early in the process if your situation is very unusual—involving fraud, for example—or if your loan is larger than the value of your property. An attorney may help you avoid losing money through a deficiency judgment if you live in a state that allows them. (See Chapter 10, "Face the Foreclosure Process," for details.)

Government agencies. The U.S. Department of Housing and Urban Development (*www.hud.gov/local/*), as mentioned above, can be especially helpful. If a government agency, such as the U.S. Department of Veterans Affairs (*www.va.gov*) or Federal Housing Administration (*www.fha.gov*), helped finance your home, it also has an interest in keeping you out of foreclosure and will offer services to that end. We'll discuss government involvement in greater detail in Chapter 7, "Take Advantage of Government Programs."

Friends and family. There's one final resource many people in trouble overlook: your friends and family. You might not have a rich uncle, and nobody has magical power over math that will make $1,000 cover a $2,000 payment. But when you invoke the wisdom of crowds, you get unexpected results. You might discover that a work colleague wants to rent your garage, that a friend's mother wants to make a long-term investment in local real estate by becoming your equity partner, or that someone's willing to make a short-term loan at better terms than you can get elsewhere. You'll get a lot of useless suggestions, of course, and might even be referred to a scammer by a gullible friend. But if you can keep up your guard and evaluate each deal on its own merits, your openness to unconventional help could have wonderful results.

Move Forward

Up to this point, we've looked at how to fix your immediate problem—that is, increasing your financial power and lowering the demands on it enough to satisfy your lender. Throughout, we've made passing references to loan terms such as *amortization* and *variable interest* and discussed possible ways that your loan might be modified or refinanced.

Now we'll take a closer look at the details of how loans actually work—the vocabulary, the market, and the math. If this is new territory, don't feel bad: many homeowners don't understand their loan's details. Some mortgage and real estate professionals may have made the problem worse by rushing you through the lending process, especially during the recent housing boom. But taking a few hours to learn the specifics could prevent you from repeating old mistakes.

As someone coming out of a foreclosure scare, you might know what it's like to get burned by a loan that's wrong for you. Your experiences may force you into a new loan; the next chapter is your guide to making sure it's the right one.

6

Understand Your Loan

Chess players are familiar with a legend about the game's origins that goes something like this. The inventor presented the first chess set to the king, who was so pleased with it that he said the inventor could claim any reward he wanted. The inventor decided to play a trick: instead of asking for lots of gold, as the king expected, he proposed that a single grain of wheat be placed on the first square of the chessboard. The next day, the king was to order two grains on the second square, then double the number of grains on each subsequent square, until he'd gone through all of the board's 64 squares, at which time the inventor would claim it all. The king laughed at the inventor's foolishness—who would prefer a few grains of wheat over gold?—and agreed.

A couple of weeks later, the royal treasurer told the king that they would soon be unable to feed the population, as the inventor's deal had bankrupted their storeroom. The first few days had gone well: one grain on the first day, two on the second, four on the third, eight on the fourth. But by the 10th day (1,024 grains) the problem had become apparent, and several bags of wheat (32,768 grains), plus a day's counting, were needed to fulfill the order on the 15th. By the 32nd day, the treasurer calculated, they would need to provide two grains of wheat for every person in the world, and completing the contract entirely would require over a hundred harvests of wheat growing on every arable square inch in the world. In one version of the story, the king calls in the inventor and offers him all the wheat—but only if he'll count it out. In another version, the king beheads him.

This is just an entertaining fable, but the math behind it is real—and, to those who don't understand it, a potential trap. For the "wheat and chessboard problem" (as mathematicians call it) is just an illustration of interest—the same interest that rules your loan. In the king's case, the interest is 200 percent per day with unusual compounding, which is about 10,000 times the typical home mortgage rate of 5 to 10 percent per year. But the concept is the same. Here's how it works.

Understand Your Loan's Math

The amount you borrow is the principal. It goes down as you pay it off and up as you borrow more money. Interest is always calculated based on your current principal by using simple multiplication. You'll remember from Chapter 3, "Rework Your Income and Expenses," that you can do math with percentages by moving the decimal point two places to the left. Therefore, annual interest on a loan of $100,000 at 6 percent is $100,000 × 0.06 = $6,000. Because there are 12 months in the year, you can figure out the monthly interest amount by dividing by 12: $6,000 / 12 = $500.

In fact, you can take out a $100,000 loan at 6 percent and pay only $500/month for it. That would be an interest-only loan, sometimes also called a straight note. You wouldn't be repaying any of the original money you owed—the principal.

But the point of most loans is that you'll pay them off eventually—they're temporary. If you pay any more than the interest amount, that extra money pays off part of the principal. As the principal shrinks, the amount you pay every month for interest decreases, even though the percentage rate stays the same.

Here's an example using the $100,000 loan at 6 percent described above ($0.005 \times$ principal = monthly interest). Let's say that instead of $500 per month, you pay $700 per month. Table 6.1 shows what the loan balance would look like every month.

You can see that a $700 payment starts off split into $500 for interest and $200 for the principal. But as the principal shrinks, so does the amount of the monthly payment that must go toward interest. So at the end of the first month, you're paying $499.00 toward the interest and $201.00 toward the principal, and so on. How long will it take to pay off this loan entirely with $700 monthly payments? Math (as programmed into a spreadsheet) gives us the answer: about 21 years. This process is called amortization, and Table 6.1 is called an amortization table.

Many years ago, American banks settled on 30 years as the standard length of time for a home mortgage. Then the question becomes: How much would you have to pay on the loan above to fully amortize—that is, pay it off—in exactly 30 years? A very complex mathematical formula involving iterations and

Table 6.1. *Reduction of Principal*

Month	Total Owed	Payment Made	Interest Portion (0.05% of Total Owed)	Principal Portion ($700 Less Interest)
1	$100,000	$700	$500.00	$200.00
2	$99,800	$700	$499.00	$201.00
3	$99,599	$700	$498.00	$202.01
4	$99,397	$700	$496.98	$203.02
5	$99,194	$700	$495.97	$204.03
6	$98,990	$700	$494.95	$205.05
7	$98,785	$700	$493.92	$206.08

exponents gives us the answer: $599.55. You can figure all this out yourself using a financial calculator. I downloaded one to my cell phone, and you can buy a dedicated calculator from Calculated Industries (*www.calculated.com*) for about $40. Better yet, dozens of Web pages host mortgage calculators, such as the ones at *http://ray.met.fsu.edu/~bret/amortize.html* and *www.amortization-calc.com*.

You'll notice from the example shown in Table 6.1 that the vast majority of your monthly payment goes toward the interest at the beginning of the loan—$500 out of $700 in the first month. That's why certain kinds of refinancing don't make much difference when done early in the loan. You haven't had that much time to reduce, or pay down, the principal. In fact, you won't have paid off half the principal until you're in your 23rd year of the 30-year loan.

Congratulations: You now understand the mechanics of your loan better than most homeowners. Let's take a look at some common clauses you might find in your mortgage—and what they could mean in case of foreclosure.

Review Your Loan's Clauses

Virtually every mortgage agreement contains an acceleration clause, which allows the lender to call the loan—that is, demand payment of the full amount—immediately if a certain event occurs, such as missing a payment.

In truth, practically every borrower does something once in a while that could trip the acceleration clause, and lenders don't invoke it for small, routine errors. But if you miss several payments, you can expect the acceleration clause hammer to fall. When that happens, the lender is basically saying, "We don't want to lend you this money anymore." Your only choices are to work out an agreement, sell the home, or refinance with another lender.

A demand clause allows the lender to call the loan for any reason at all, even no reason. Loans with a demand clause are especially onerous, because the lender could capriciously decide to raise your interest rate (if permitted by the agreement) and invoke the demand clause, in essence saying, "Either start paying me more interest or pay the full loan amount right now." The Truth-in-Lending Disclosure Statement that accompanies every loan (which we'll describe later) contains a checkbox to show whether a loan contains a demand clause. Read your loan with special care if it's checked. However, some lenders mistakenly check it, confusing *demand clause* with *acceleration clause,* so the fact that that box is checked isn't a sure sign that the loan contains a demand clause.

The alienation clause, also known as the due-on-sale clause or anti-assumption clause, is a special kind of acceleration clause that says you have to pay back the full amount when you sell or otherwise transfer ("alienate") your home. Most mortgage agreements these days have an alienation clause, unless the loan is assumable, in which case an assumption clause will give details on how to transfer the loan to a new buyer. Assumable loans are uncommon in times of low interest rates, such as we're experiencing now; those that exist have additional clauses that spell out how the loan will be assumed when the first owner sells.

An assumable loan allows your home's buyer to continue the loan that you hold. Buyers like them because they avoid the hassle and fees involved in getting a new loan. But assumable loans can be tricky, and you should be especially wary of any foreclosure "rescue" operation that says it will assume your loans. First of all, the assumption doesn't always let you off the hook completely: many assumption clauses give the seller—you—secondary liability for the loan. That means that if the buyer fails to pay it, you have to, even though you don't own the home anymore! You might be able to take certain steps to protect yourself in an assumption, such as filing a Substitution of Liability form, but now we're entering the realm of law, where the advice of a local attorney is an absolute necessity.

Also, avoid any rescue plan that makes the purchase "subject to" your existing loan. The buyer might call such a deal an "assumption" of the existing loan, but don't be fooled: the phrase *subject to* means that the new owner takes on *no* liability for the loan at all. You're still on the hook for 100 percent of it.

Some scammers attempt to hide the fact that you're transferring ownership of the property from yourself to someone else, because they want the original loan to remain in effect. In other words, they want to avoid invoking the alienation clause. This is a likely sign of a scam: do it, and you could find yourself not only owing all the money but also being the target of a fraud lawsuit from the lender.

Subordination clauses are rare and generally to the advantage of the borrower. A loan with such a clause can be made lower in priority to loans made later. We'll discuss loan priority further in Chapter 10, "Face the Foreclosure Process," but in essence, a lower priority makes the loan less valuable to the lender.

Here's an example. Say you buy a $350,000 home with a $50,000 down payment and a $300,000 loan. The loan contains a subordination clause. You later need more money and find a lender who'll lend you a further $50,000 secured by your home—but only if the first loan becomes subordinate to the second loan. You sign the papers and now have two loans: a new "first" loan for $50,000 and a "second" loan (which used to be the "first") for $300,000. Then you lose your job and have to sell the home; however, prices have fallen, and you can only get $325,000 for it. The $50,000 loan gets paid off first, followed by the second, $300,000 loan. However, there's only $275,000 ($325,000 − $50,000) left to pay off the second lender, who has to just take what it can get. If the $300,000 loan hadn't contained a subordination clause, that lender would have gotten paid off in full.

Why would you, as someone facing foreclosure, have to know about subordination clauses? Well, you may be approached by someone who says they'll buy your home—if you front them some part of the price in what's called a seller-carryback loan or owner-financing arrangement. This person might even make the deal seem especially attractive by offering a better-than-market price, for example $400,000 for a $350,000 house.

Here's how the scam works. Let's say you still owe $50,000 on your mortgage. The scammer puts down $100,000, which allows you to pay off your existing mortgage and pocket $50,000 yourself. In return, you "carry" or "take back" a loan for the remainder of the price; that is, the amount the buyers still owe you, or $400,000 − $100,000 = $300,000. They then arrange to take out as big a loan as they can get from an institutional lender, such as a bank, In some cases, this loan will be as much as the full purchase price of the home, or $400,000. This step requires some fraud on their part, as no bank would loan them that much money if they knew about the money they owe you via the seller-carryback loan.

The scammers complete the transaction, now owing $400,000 to the bank and $300,000 to you—a total of $700,000 on a home that's only worth $350,000 on the market. They then take the bank's money and disappear. The bank forecloses on them, and you've received only their down payment ($100,000) in exchange for the $350,000 market value − $50,000 mortgage = $300,000 equity you sold. You've lost $200,000; the bank, which can only get $350,000 for a home on which it loaned $400,000, has lost $50,000. Your $200,000 plus the bank's $50,000 plus the home's sale price of $350,000 equals the $700,000 the scammers borrowed.

If you had trouble following that, don't worry. The important thing to remember is that you should *never* agree to a subordination clause or, for that matter, any seller-carryback loan, without independent legal advice and a complete understanding of the deal. Subordination clauses have their place. For example, they're common in sales of raw land, where the seller knows that the buyer will eventually have to take out a construction loan to improve it. But for ordinary home sales? Forget 'em.

Finally, find out whether your mortgage contains a prepayment penalty clause. These are often written into loans that give you an especially good deal for the first few years—for example, if you were granted a low teaser interest rate. Lenders make money on a loan that lacks a prepayment penalty only if you hold onto it for a sufficiently long period. Loans with prepayment penalties guarantee the lender's profit even if you leave it earlier than expected. State laws vary regarding how big prepayment penalties can be, but they can end up costing you thousands of dollars. That's fine if the foreclosure workout plan justifies this expense, but it can be a terrible shock if you're not aware of it.

Be Prepared to Pay Fees for a New Loan

You may face a few loan fees and costs if your foreclosure work-out involves getting a new loan. This list isn't exhaustive—the mortgage industry is always coming up with new ways to frame such costs, either to be fairer to borrowers or more profitable to themselves. Here are some of the more common ones.

Mortgage Insurance

Mortgage insurance is a monthly cost that's required when the lender believes the foreclosure of your home might not repay the amount you owe. The industry standard is to charge mortgage insurance, or MI, if the loan amount is greater than 80 percent of the purchase price or assessed value, whichever is lower.

Why 80 percent? Lenders know that their costs to sell your home after foreclosure are likely to be 5 to 10 percent and are betting that the home won't lose more than 10 percent of its value in addition; that is, a total loss of more than 20 percent. So let's say you buy a $200,000 home with $160,000 (80 percent) from the lender, then go into foreclosure. Assuming you've paid nothing to reduce the principal—as with an interest-only loan—the lender only cares that sale of the property gets back the $160,000. On this $200,000 home, a typical 8 percent cost of sale (for real estate agents, paperwork, escrow, appraisers, and so forth) is $16,000; therefore, the lender needs $160,000 + $16,000 = $176,000 to break even. Some very unusual circumstances would need to be in play for the lender to be unable to sell a $200,000 home for $176,000, so it feels safe making the loan without mortgage insurance.

But what if you need to borrow more than 80 percent of the home's value? When the loan-to-value (LTV) ratio goes higher, the lender doesn't feel as secure that it would be able to make back its money in a foreclosure sale and will demand that you pay for some form of mortgage insurance to insure against *its* risk of loss. That's right: You're paying for insurance that only benefits the lender! Furthermore, you don't usually get to choose the insurer—the lender does that. With MI, you can borrow 95 percent of the purchase price ($190,000 for that $200,000 home) or more. If the lender only gets $180,000 from its sale, the insurer pays it the difference; in this case, that's $190,000 loan – $180,000 sale proceeds = $10,000.

Avoiding mortgage insurance. There is a way to get out of paying mortgage insurance: get a completely different second loan for any amount borrowed above the bottom portion of 80 percent. That second loan could come from the same lender, and in fact, many lenders offer packages that include not only the first loan for the bottom portion but a second loan for anything above that. This second loan is usually on a shorter term than the bigger, first loan. The idea is that you'll pay it off quickly and eventually only have one loan—the bottom one.

This loan for the top portion will have terms that aren't as favorable as the first, bottom-portion loan, but that makes sense: it's not as well secured as the first loan. Continuing in our example, let's say you refinance that $200,000 home with an 80 percent ($160,000) bottom loan and a 15 percent ($30,000) top loan for a total of 95 percent ($190,000). You go into foreclosure, and the lender only gets $185,000 for the house after paying the costs of sale. The first, "bottom" loan of $160,000 gets paid off in full, but the second, "top" loan only gets $185,000 – $160,000 = $25,000 paid of its $30,000 amount. That's the risk the top lender takes, and it compensates by charging higher fees or a higher interest rate.

As always, compare mortgage insurance with the second-loan option by running the numbers to compare total loan costs and—most importantly for someone having trouble meeting the payments—the size of the check you'll have to send off every month.

Points

Points are an amount of money you give to the lender at the beginning of a loan in exchange for a reduced interest rate. The cost of a point is, simply, 1 percent of the loan amount, so for a $160,000 loan, 1 point = $160,000 × 0.01 = $1,600. Points are essentially prepaid interest, and tax authorities treat them that way. Many well-advertised loans require payment of points, a fact that uneducated borrowers gloss over—until they're surprised by it at the closing table. (The word *point* seems so insignificant—nothing in the world could be smaller than a zero-dimensional "point," right?) When offered a refinancing deal to get out of foreclosure, give points the weight they deserve in your decision. A calculator at the Mortgage Professor's website (*www.mtgprofessor.com/calculatorsOriginalMenu.htm*) can help you decide whether points are worth the cost, based on the number of points, the interest discount you get by buying them, and how long you plan to hold the loan.

Other Standard Fees

Lending money is a complicated affair. Depending on your situation and where you live, it could involve appraisers, mortgage brokers, attorneys, credit-reporting bureaus, and insurance companies in addition to your lender. Guess who pays all these people?

In addition to points, here are some typical one-time closing charges and who gets them:

- appraisal (appraiser)
- attorneys (themselves)
- credit reports (credit bureau)
- homeowner's insurance (insurer)
- inspections (individual inspectors)
- land survey (individual inspectors)
- loan application fees (lender)
- loan origination fees (mortgage broker)
- recording fees (county government)
- title insurance (title insurance company)
- transfer taxes (state and local governments)

Some other up-front charges are actually prepayments or for recurring items; that is, they're not service fees but rather interest charges and the like. The per diem interest charge is for days that you hold the loan before the next month starts. (Yep, they calculate the loan down to the *day*. When you're talking about hundreds of thousands of dollars, it makes a difference!) Impound accounts hold prepayments for property taxes and hazard insurance that you make with each mortgage payment. The lender usually requires such accounts because its security could disappear or lose value if you fail to pay for those items.

Junk fees. There's frequent discussion about mortgage junk fees—that is, fees tacked on to a loan that go straight into a lender's pocket, don't appear to have any benefit to the borrower, and pay for work that's either not performed or typically part of lender costs. Arguments abound on which fees are "junk" and which aren't. Is a "warehouse fee" valid if, in fact, the lender has to pay someone to store your files for the legally required period? What about mail and shipping charges? Printouts of long documents that were sent by email? What's a reasonable charge per page?

You can always challenge costs that you think are junk fees, and you might get some of them removed. But to be honest, the lender more often will tell you to take it or leave it—at the signing table, when you're in a poor position to leave it. Try to get an estimated list of charges as far ahead of time so you can check and "correct" any fees that you feel are invalid.

Do You Have a Mortgage or a Deed of Trust?

Throughout this book, we've used the term mortgage, but now it can be told: if your home is in one of the western states, chances are you don't have a mortgage at all but rather a deed of trust paired with a promissory note. There's very little practical difference between the two, except at the loan's origination—and if a foreclosure process begins.

A mortgage is the simplest form of loan, involving only you (the mortgagor) and the lender (the mortgagee). The mortgage is an all-in-one document that gets recorded with the county government, making it a public record. It spells out both the details of the loan itself and how the loan is secured by your home. If you default and the lender wants to repossess your home, a judicial foreclosure is usually necessary; that is, the lender has to file a lawsuit and go through a court process before the home can be sold and the lender can recapture its money.

A promissory note and deed of trust is a three-party instrument: There's a trustee in addition to you (the trustor) and the lender (the beneficiary). The terms of your loan—the loan amount, interest rate, penalties, and so on—are written into a fairly short promissory note, which is not put in the public record. The deed of trust, which *is* recorded, clarifies all the rights the lender/ beneficiary has in your home, including its right to repossess and sell it. For legal reasons, these powers actually vest with the trustee, not the beneficiary, and the trustee (typically a title or escrow company) oversees the foreclosure process.

Because deeds of trust and some mortgages contain a power-of-sale clause, the lender doesn't need to go to court to perform a foreclosure on those instruments. Such nonjudicial foreclosures are faster, cheaper, and more reliable for the lender. (We'll discuss the details in Chapter 10, "Face the Foreclosure Process.")

Move Forward

I hope this chapter has given you a better understanding of your existing loan. But more importantly, I hope it gives you guidance in whatever loan you take (if any) to get out of foreclosure—and how to avoid repeating any past errors.

With luck and hard work, you've now settled with your lender, set up ways to pay your mortgage in the future, and avoided the actual foreclosure process. But sometimes there simply is no workout: the lender is going to foreclose. There are still some things you can do to stop the process once it starts, but even if you can't, just knowing what's going to happen is half the battle.

Take Advantage of Government Programs

People who have never gone through a real estate transaction often ask why they're so complicated. After all (they say), they want to sell their house and I want to buy it: What else is there to talk about? With some discussion, however, they quickly come to see the need for lenders (and their regulations); a bit more, and they understand the special complications of owning an immovable, eternal object. But government involvement in real estate transactions is more complicated, if only because the government is involved in hidden ways at virtually every step, from before you purchase until after you sell. While such oversight sometimes leads to confusion and annoyances, it also supports programs and opportunities that help you avoid or minimize the effects of foreclosure.

Governments in effect *are* the lands they rule: without the ability to seize and control land in their domains, they have no power. And historically, land has been "owned" exclusively by the government, with various rights licensed to private parties, such as homeowners. That's as true in modern-day America as it was in the feudal days of kings and serfs. Do something with "your" land that's against government policy, or fail to do something that's required of you, and you'll lose it. In fact, the word *real* in *real estate* doesn't mean "actual" but is instead derived from *royal*—in other words, it's land owned by (and protected by) the "royal" family (government).

National, state, and local governments are highly motivated to encourage stable and profitable land use in their jurisdictions. As the National Association of REALTORS® says in the preamble to its Code of Ethics and Standards of Practice, "Under all is the land. Upon its wise utilization and widely allocated ownership depend the survival and growth of free institutions and of our civilization." In the United States, "widely allocated ownership" has translated into radical policies that encourage individual homeownership.

The upshot is this: the government wants you to keep your home. If you can't solve the problem yourself—and even if you can—let it help you.

The national government agency most closely involved in fore-closure issues is the Department of Housing and Urban Development (HUD). The two departments within HUD of most interest to homeowners are the Federal Housing Administration (FHA), which has several programs that encourage home ownership, and the Office of Federal Housing Enterprise Oversight (OFHEO), which oversees the two government-sponsored entities described below, Fannie Mae and Freddie Mac. Other agencies include the Federal Trade Commission (FTC), which regulates advertising and some credit issues; the Federal Deposit Insurance Corporation

(FDIC), which insures bank deposits and has some enforcement powers; the Department of Justice (DOJ), which maintains a list of credit counseling resources as part of its Trustee Program; and the Internal Revenue Service (IRS), which stands ready to guide you on tax issues related to foreclosure.

In addition, some private organizations work so closely with the government that they're considered quasi-governmental agencies. Two of these figure large in housing issues: Fannie Mae (the popular name for the Federal National Mortgage Association, or FNMA), and Freddie Mac (the Federal Home Loan Mortgage Corporation, or FHLMC). Both of these are government-sponsored enterprises (GSE), created through U.S. legislation to stabilize the mortgage market by giving lenders a venue in which they can sell or buy loans they've made to homeowners. To be eligible for Fannie Mae and Freddie Mac programs, loans must conform to those organizations' guidelines, and their lenders must follow certain procedures—many of which are designed to help keep homeowners in their homes. Because most home loans are "conforming," there's a good chance the actions of these GSEs can help you, albeit indirectly.

The Four Categories of Government Help

Government programs that will help you in foreclosure fall into four categories:

1. *Regulations.* More good news: Despite massive political donations and lobbying from lenders, finance legislation remains fairly friendly to homeowners. Governments generally believe that the lender is more sophisticated—

and therefore more likely to cause abuse—than the borrower and create laws accordingly. You might feel tricked into signing a contract that's beyond your understanding; but because of numerous laws, the contract itself has to spell everything out, and its clauses are highly regulated to prevent systematic abuse. Lender regulations are so numerous and complex that an industry has arisen to help finance professionals follow them all. The "standard package" of forms and guidelines for lenders sold at AllRegs (*www.allregs.com*) comprises *thousands* of pages—and the "premium" and "platinum" packages are even bigger.

Having said that, enforcement for these laws often falls to you, the consumer. Only your own knowledge and vigilance will save you if believe you're the victim of illegal activity.

2. *Advice.* "Talk is cheap"—cheaper than paying for things, certainly. But the fact that advice is free doesn't necessarily make it any less useful. While government agencies are no substitute for the services of an individual attorney, homeowners in foreclosure typically are, by definition, having trouble paying the bills. Further, advice received through government resources is "official," in the sense that it reflects current laws and policies. Errors occur, of course, but government-approved advice is at least closer to the source.

3. *Direct assistance.* By this I mean money or benefits that go directly to you without being filtered through a third party, such as a lender. In our "pull yourself up by your bootstraps" culture, direct assistance is somewhat thin on the ground: in short, the government's not going to pay your mortgage. But some assistance does exist in unusual (and somewhat complicated) forms such as tax breaks and loan assumptions. A special kind of direct assistance—bankruptcy—will be discussed in Chapter 9, "If All Else Fails . . . Declare Bankruptcy."

4. *Indirect assistance.* These programs work by giving financial power to lenders and others involved in mortgage finance, with the idea that doing so will enable them to make and support bigger, better, and more flexible loans. The best-known of these programs involve mortgage insurance—that is, protection for lenders in case the homeowner can't pay the mortgage.

Regulations That Protect You

As I write this, Congress is circulating a bill to address the most visible examples of predatory lending, whereby mortgage brokers have taken advantage of borrowers' ignorance, desperation, or trust to sell loans that are either overpriced or designed to fail. Another recently passed bill removes a tax liability from most homeowners who sell their property through a short sale. Meanwhile, a White House proposal is trying to freeze the rates on some adjustable-rate loans to forestall the shock of their eventual increase. As housing's postboom deflation has continued, government has more than ever perceived a need for regulation—much of it targeted to help homeowners who bought in the past five years.

We won't cover legislation that's still unsettled; even if passed, some of it wouldn't become law for months or even years after you read this. (A counselor can give you the current status of such laws and advice on how they might apply to your situation.)

The most important regulation of interest to a homeowner facing foreclosure is the Truth-in-Lending Act, passed in 1968. It ordered lenders to put together a statement for every qualified loan, giving details on certain frequently misunderstood parts of the lending contract. This statement is called the Truth-in-Lending (TIL) form, or Regulation Z, after the section of federal law that contains it (Code of Federal Regulations, Part 226). The U.S. government requires lenders to give borrowers a copy of this single-page document for most extensions of consumer credit, including any refinancing you perform to get out of foreclosure. If you don't receive this statement—or don't agree with its contents—question the loan.

From top to bottom, here's what some of the less-obvious fields mean:

■ *Annual percentage rate (APR).* You may be surprised to see a different number here from the one quoted you by the mortgage broker: that's because the APR includes all mortgage fees that you pay at the loan's origination, in addition to the principal. For example, let's say you're promised a $100,000 loan at 6 percent interest for 30 years but the total finance charges are $3,000. To calculate the effective APR, lenders add that $3,000 to the total you'll spend on the loan over its period and do some fairly complex math to determine that $3,000 adds as much cost to your loan as a 0.278 percent rate increase. Therefore, the effective APR is 6% + 0.278% = 6.278%. The shorter the loan, the more significant the up-front fees. For example, if you took out the loan above for only 15 years, the effective APR would be 6.465 percent; for five years, it would be a whopping 7.236 percent. The mortgage calculator at *www.dinkytown. net/java/MortgageApr.html* lets you play with the numbers to find your own APR.

■ *Finance charge.* This part is a big shock to many people who aren't aware of the cost of credit. It tells you how much you'll pay in interest, mortgage insurance, and other fees over the course of the loan. This amount is much higher than most people expect. In our example above, you'd pay a little over $120,000 in interest and fees for the $100,000 loan over 30 years—and that doesn't pay down the principal at all!

- *Amount financed.* This number is almost always smaller than the nominal loan amount, because it doesn't include certain closing fees, such as points paid to reduce your interest rate. In other words, it's the amount of money that's going toward the cost of your home.

- *Payment schedule.* This section spells out how much your monthly payment will be, including future increases in the case of a variable-interest loan.

The rest of the form is mostly a series of check boxes and fill-in-the-blank spaces for a variety of details of varying importance to your loan, such as whether your loan has the aforementioned demand clause (sometimes called a "demand feature" on the form), whether you'd like to buy various types of insurance from the lender, if the loan has a prepayment penalty, and whether the loan's assumable. You may have glossed over these points when you bought the home, but they could become important during your foreclosure workout, so re-read the form to make sure a proposed solution is actually possible according to the terms of your loan. If you have time, of course it's a good idea to read through your original loan in its entirety, but for the time-starved (and who isn't?), the Truth-in-Lending statement is an adequate summary.

Let's say that you read the Truth-in-Lending statement and signed on the dotted line, only to find something bad about the loan the next morning. Believe it or not, you have three business days to cancel the contract! This right of rescission is part of the federal Truth-in-Lending law and is good for any refinance loan that's secured by the home you occupy. The lender has to return any money you've handed over, although you won't get back money paid to a third party for the loan, such as an appraiser or credit-reporting agency.

Good Advice from Trusted Sources

As discussed at length in Chapter 4, "Learn How to Avoid Scams," all sorts of characters will crawl out of the woodwork to "advise" you on your foreclosure—not all of them truly helpful or even legitimate. There's one source you can count on: the U.S. Department of Housing and Urban Development's list of approved housing counselors. You can search the list at *www.hud.gov/offices/hsg/sfh/hcc/hcs.cfm,* and details on how exactly the department approves these counselors is at *www.hud.gov/offices/hsg/sfh/hcc/hcc_home.cfm.* And, of course, *www.hud.gov/foreclosure/* is the easy-to-remember link for all HUD programs; 1-800-569-4287 is the department's toll-free number.

Two other organizations that provide directories of counselors are Fannie Mae (*www.mortgagecontent.net/findCounselorApplication/fanniemae/findCounselor.jsp*) and the U.S. Department of Justice (*www.usdoj.gov/ust/eo/bapcpa/ccde/*).

What sort of advice can you expect from these agencies? That depends on the services they offer, which HUD puts in the following categories:

- Predatory lending

- Marketing and outreach initiatives

- Homebuyer education programs

- Renters' assistance

- Postpurchase counseling

- Home equity conversion mortgage counseling

- Fair housing assistance

- Home improvement and rehabilitation counseling

- Mortgage delinquency and default resolution counseling

- Loss mitigation

- Mobility and relocation counseling

- Services for homeless

- Money debt management

These agencies sometimes charge small fees—$30 or less—for counseling sessions, classes, and the like. There may be additional fees if you decide to use the mediation services that some of them offer.

But these fees are fairly small compared to the value of the information you're likely to get. In fact, the fees don't even come close to covering these agencies' costs. Guess where the rest of the money comes from? Governments and individual donations pay for some services, but much of their funding comes from— believe it or not—lenders themselves. Once again, lenders know that they're going to lose out on some loans: they just want such losses to be as small as possible. They believe that an educated borrower is much more likely to handle a potential foreclosure in a controlled, reasonable, manageable way. Funding counseling agencies is a bargain compared to losses caused by the actions of panicked borrowers.

So what will the advice be like? If all you have is a simple question, you might get an answer right over the phone. But if you need more, the counselor will ask you to schedule a longer phone or face-to-face meeting. The agency's website (linked from HUD's listings) may have forms the counselor wants you to fill out. Fortunately, the information you put together in Chapter 2, "Get a Handle on Your Situation," puts you way ahead of the herd: all you need to do is copy your information onto the agency's form.

Some of that information might be highly confidential, and you might rightly be worried about its abuse. But you have a big fighter in your corner if you think the agency is cheating you: HUD itself. These agencies count on HUD's referrals for business, so the threat of delisting gives your complaint leverage.

Other government websites that provide foreclosure advice include the following:

- The Federal Reserve Board (*www.federalreserve.gov/pubs/foreclosure/default.htm*)

- The U.S. Department of Veterans Affairs (*www.homeloans.va.gov/paytrbl.htm*)

- Numerous local and state government sites. Try a search for "foreclosure" and the name of your state at *www.usasearch.gov.*

Finally, the organization NeighborWorks America has the government stamp of approval as a "federally affiliated organization." It maintains a Center for Foreclosure Solutions at *www.nw.org*.

Direct Assistance: Money in Your Pocket

The biggest kind of direct governmental assistance for homeowners in foreclosure is in the form of tax breaks that, unfortunately, don't kick in until *after* you've given up your home. Nonetheless, they're worth discussing here.

The first is the federal capital gains exemption granted to homeowners who have lived in their current home for at least 24 months of the past 5 years. Normally, any profit made from sale of a home is taxed as capital gains, generally at a rate of 15 percent. If you aren't able to keep your home, you'll either end up giving it back to the bank (as a deed in lieu of foreclosure) or selling it. If your home has appreciated in value, the profit that comes from its sale is theoretically taxable. However, the capital gains exemption allows you to keep up to $250,000 as an individual, or $500,000 as a married couple, free of capital gains taxes. This exemption removes a substantial barrier to selling, as it directly saves $1,500 on every $10,000 you might earn from such a sale.

The second kind of tax relief is found in the homestead exemptions offered by state governments. These provide the ability to protect some part of your home's value from creditors and property taxes. They vary widely from state to state: an online guide is at *www.assetprotectionbook.com/homestead_exemptions.htm*.

Another kind of direct assistance is available to homeowners who have loans that are insured by the FHA. The agency provides a wide range of programs:

- Administration of a Partial Claim, in which the FHA actually gives you an interest-free loan of the money you need to get caught up with your current lender. You don't have to pay back this money until you either sell the property or pay off your original debt. Details on the program are somewhat technical and intended for the lender (who initiates the Partial Claim process). You can read a bit about them at *www.hud.gov/offices/hsg/sfh/nsc/faqpc.cfm*. A call to your lender, local FHA office, or HUD-approved counseling agency is a much better way to figure out whether you're qualified.

- A stay of foreclosure for 90 days as disaster relief for those whose homes are in a ZIP code defined by the Federal Emergency Management Agency (FEMA) as a "disaster area." In addition, many lenders will forgo late charges and other fees.

See *www.fha.gov/foreclosure/* for a list of all relevant FHA programs.

If you or your spouse is on active military service or bought your home using a loan guaranteed by the Department of Veterans Affairs, you have additional resources:

- The Servicemembers Civil Relief Act (SCRA) of 2003 (formerly the Soldiers' and Sailors' Civil Relief Act of 1940, or SSCRA) does two things for active servicemembers: it forces lenders to lower your interest rate to no more than 6 percent during your active service, and it prevents them from foreclosing without a court order. Further details on the program are at *www.fha.gov/foreclosure/SCRA.cfm*.

■ If you bought your home with a VA-guaranteed loan, that loan might be assumable—that is, the person who purchases your home can take it over. If you decide to sell, the loan's assumability could help you get a higher price.

■ You might have to sell your home for less than its loan value—a short sale. Short sales are described in Chapter 8, "Sell Before the Pain Starts." When you have a VA-backed loan, it's called a compromise sale and carries with it special requirements. For details, call the Department of Veterans Affairs at 1-800-827-1000 or search for a local office at *www.va.gov*.

Indirect Assistance That Helps Those Who Help You

The FHA provides an enormous wealth of guidance for lenders whose loans are insured through an FHA program. While most of it is highly technical and irrelevant to individual homeowners, you may be able to help your lender find ways to give you relief—or avoid acting in illegal ways—by poring over the documents in the FHA's National Servicing Center (*www.hud.gov/offices/hsg/sfh/nsc/nschome.cfm*). One document there, entitled "Treble Damages for Failure to Engage in Loss Mitigation," quotes the law that penalizes your lender if it doesn't try to make a workout plan with you.

The Federal Home Loan Mortgage Corporation, commonly known as Freddie Mac, actually gives small amounts of money (up to $1,100) to lenders who successfully work out qualified loans with delinquent borrowers. If your lender is a bank or other financial institution, it is almost certainly already aware of the program; if it's a private lender (such as a relative or the home's previous owner), there's a good chance it doesn't, and this "found money" will be another good reason to modify your current loan and let you keep your home. Details are at *www.freddiemac. com/service/factsheets/woinc.html*.

Another Freddie Mac program, for "superior foreclosure time-line performance," could actually harm you, as it encourages loan servicers to process delinquencies in a "timely" fashion; i.e., as soon as possible. Ironically, this incentive could make a lender *less* likely to be patient with you; fortunately, the incentives are comparatively small, topping out at $8 per day.

Move Forward

We've focused on programs run by the federal government, primarily because assistance provided by state and local governments could easily fill several books by itself. For example, the California Department of Veterans Affairs offers a loan program for veterans who live in that state, while the Connecticut Housing Finance Authority has an "emergency mortgage assistance program" that provides direct assistance for homeowners facing temporary problems. Further, local phenomena (such as wildfires and floods) sometimes inspire regional legislation to help residents avoid losing their homes, while local governments and nongovernmental organizations may offer additional programs. The best way to learn about them is to follow links from HUD's local directory of resources at *www.hud.gov/local/* to a nonprofit counseling agency, which will be in touch with all the help local organizations can bring to bear.

By now, you've looked over your finances, talked to your lender, considered options from other parties, and gotten the best counseling you can find. Perhaps you haven't found a solution that works yet, or maybe you've decided that staying in your home will simply be too troublesome or expensive. That means selling, and obviously you want to get the most money you can—but within a time frame that will avoid problems with your lender. No single sales method is right for every situation, so we'll briefly explore them all in the next chapter.

Sell Before the
Pain Starts

I'm going to let you in on a little secret: even though this book is called *Save Your Home*, sometimes your best course of action is just to let it go. And while your home may represent a great past, selling it begins your future. As the Roman philosopher Seneca wrote (and rock group Semisonic quoted in song), "Every new beginning comes from some other beginning's end."

There are two ways to sell a home: for the fast buck or for the last buck. In "fast buck" sales, you're seeking to get out of trouble as soon as possible, and any profit you make is gravy. The "last buck" scenario is for people who have enough time and resources to get the highest possible price. As a homeowner facing foreclosure, you probably fall somewhere on the "fast buck" side of the spectrum. Just how far depends on the stage of foreclosure, your financial resources, how much time your lender will give you to sell, and whether you're considering bankruptcy (see Chapter 9, "If All Else Fails . . . Declare Bankruptcy").

The amount of your profit—or whether the sales price will even cover your debts—depends on the size of your equity in the home, which you might remember defined in Chapter 2, "Get a Handle on Your Situation," as "the amount of money you'd walk away with if you sold your home." The trick is that the amount you owe can be changed in some circumstances by negotiation with the lender, as we saw in Chapter 5, "Call for Help." Even more nebulous is your home's "market value," which varies depending on how you sell and to whom; in any case, you won't know the actual number until *after* the sale is complete. Plus, you'll have to deduct your costs of sale of 2 to 10 percent from the equity to arrive at a final profit figure.

The way you choose to sell your home strongly affects how much profit you'll get and the risks you'll take to get it. The three main methods are these:

1. *To a quick-sale buyer.* Quick-sale buyers are typically experienced investors who offer an all-cash deal (i.e., needing no new loans) and a quick close. They won't require as many formalities as a "traditional" buyer and, in fact, might buy your home without ever setting foot in it. Their actual sale price will be much lower than what you could get on the open market, but in exchange, you get a definite sale and quick exit.

2. *By yourself as a "for sale by owner (FSBO)."* The main advantage to selling your home yourself, as a for-sale-by-owner, is that you could save as much as 4 to 6 percent of the sales price that the two agents would claim. While there are substantial pitfalls to running a FSBO—which we'll discuss below—it's hard to argue with savings that could be as high as $24,000 for a $400,000 home. (In practice,

you're more likely to save only half of that or less because the buyer's agent will still need to be paid.)

3. *With the help of a real estate agent.* A real estate agent's job is multifaceted. It requires knowledge of finance, marketing, decorating, sales, contract negotiation, law, architecture, and construction. All of this comes together to provide what I think is an agent's most valuable function: a reality check. Your agents will examine the market as it actually is, then set a price and marketing plan that's likely to sell your home in the time you specify. Ultimately, they have no control over the market; they can only make educated guesses. Therefore, their education and experience are paramount, and for that you'll typically pay 2 to 3 percent of the final sales price.

In any case, you'll need the cooperation of your lender to sell if your loan's in default—that is, if you've missed any payments or the lender has called the loan for any other reason. Further, you'll have to abide by certain legal requirements no matter how you sell. These requirements vary from place to place. In my home town of San Francisco, for example, buyers expect a "Supplemental Transfer Disclosure Statement," which forces you to share what you know about certain additional aspects of the property.

Before beginning, calculate an estimated seller's proceeds sheet. This is the amount of money you expect to have in your pocket (if any) when the sale is complete. Figure 8.1 is a form that outlines some of the bigger expenses. (Not all will be applicable to you, as they vary from region to region, as does whether the seller or buyer pays them.) When you're done, you'll have a clearer picture of the sales price you truly need to pay off your loans. If the sales price offered ultimately gives you a negative

Figure 8.1. *Seller's Proceeds Sheet*

Estimated sale price		$ _____
First mortgage	–	$ _____
Second mortgage	–	$ _____
Other monetary liens	–	$ _____
Total gross equity		$ _____

Sale Expenses	**Typical Amount**		
Listing agent's commission	2%–3% of price		$ _____
Selling agent's commission	2%–3% of price		$ _____
Attorney's fees	$300–$2,000		$ _____
Escrow charges	$100–$600	+	$ _____
Title insurance	$500–$2,500	+	$ _____
Transfer tax	0.01%–1.5%	+	$ _____
Real estate taxes still due	varies	+	$ _____
Appraisal	$100–$600	+	$ _____
Inspection fees	$50–$1,000	+	$ _____
Presale repairs	varies	+	$ _____
Other		+	$ _____
Total sale expenses			$ _____
Total gross equity			$ _____
Total sale expenses		–	$ _____
Estimated seller's proceeds			$ _____

bottom line, you'd probably be better off giving your lender a deed in lieu (see Chapter 5, "Call for Help"), which would save you the substantial costs of sale.

One of the toughest parts of selling a home is setting the price. The best way to do that is to look at other homes, similar to yours and in the same area, that have sold in the past year. These are known as comparable properties or simply comps; a report that measures all the comps against your home is known as a comparative market analysis (CMA). Real estate agents can prepare a CMA for you in exchange for the expectation that you'll let them sell the property. If you decide to sell your home yourself or want to compare its market value to the amount a quick-sale buyer is offering, you can get a general idea of value using the automated valuation model websites listed in Chapter 2, "Get a Handle on Your Situation."

Sell to a Quick-Sale Buyer

As you start to get into financial trouble, those "Sell your home for cash!" billboards will start to look awfully tempting. And if your troubles become public (through a notice of default or lender's court complaint), those temptations will swarm around you through phone calls, direct mail, and even people knocking on your door. Friends and family you haven't seen in years may appear to add their proposals to the mix. While the pitches may vary, their propositions are the same: in exchange for your home, they'll get you out of trouble and possibly give you some money as well. By themselves, these deals aren't objectionable and, in fact, may be preferable to selling the "traditional" way.

But these preforeclosure buyers aren't trying to help you out of the goodness of their hearts. They're looking to make money by paying you a low price, then reselling the property at a higher price. Such buyers are typically looking for a price that's at least 20 percent below the open-market value to pay for their risk (in case they can't sell it), time, expenses, and profit.

While many preforeclosure buyers are knowledgeable and experienced, the field of foreclosure investing has been marketed as a get-rich-quick scheme through dozens of books of greatly varying quality. As a result, some of the people who approach you will be inexperienced, ignorant of how to consummate the deal, and even criminal-minded. (A fair number of these books recommend practices that are illegal, including some of those described in Chapter 4, "Learn How to Avoid Scams.") Certainly resist the temptation to call anyone who advertises by using spam (unsolicited email); by posting "bandit signs" in median strips, along the highway, or on private property; or any other illegal method. They're telling you through their actions that they're willing to break the law in the name of greed.

Here are some rules to managing quick-sale offers:

- *Remember Essential Truth #3: You have options.* Some quick-sale buyers will tell you that they're your only solution and that "no one else will give you this deal." That's just a sales technique intended to make you feel helpless, and it's probably not true. Treat such statements as a red flag.

- *Always keep an eye on the bottom line.* Use the seller's proceeds worksheet above to test out every proposed deal, keeping in mind that a quick-sale buyer won't incur some of the expenses that a "traditional" buyer would. (For example, the quick-sale buyer might not need title insurance or an appraisal.) If you have any doubts, ask the buyer to go over the sheet with you.

- *Avoid confusing deals.* The investor may offer nonmonetary goodies (like a car) or benefits that are hard to measure (such as a share in a business). If it's not money, ignore it; if it doesn't pay off your debts and put cash in your pocket, question its value.

- *Be ready to walk away.* One common trick of unscrupulous buyers is to promise you one thing, then deliver another. Read the final contract before you sign it and ignore any verbal promises. If the written contract doesn't match what you discussed, walk away.

I actually think a homeowner in foreclosure can do very well selling to preforeclosure investors—but not the ones who solicit you. They're just good at marketing, and if they reached you, they probably also reached many other homeowners in distress. They can therefore pick and choose only those deals that are most advantageous to them—and possibly most disadvantageous to you.

Instead, proactively post ads in forums where real estate investors hang out and that permit such postings. Better yet, contact whoever runs local investor meetings to find out how you could advertise your deal to its members: some have an announcement period where members are happy to hear from distressed homeowners. Remember, your problem is their profit! A list of real estate investor clubs is at *www.reiclub.com/real-estate-clubs.php*.

When you become proactive in finding a buyer for your home, you move away from the realm of "quick-sale bait" and into the world of traditional sales. So let's take a look at the range of ways you can sell your home yourself for the most money.

Sell Your Home Yourself

Visit any large bookstore's real estate section, and you'll be confronted with a wall full of "sell your own home" books that are full of details on marketing, regulations, escrow, and repairs. This short section can't hope to compete with those weighty tomes; rather, it's intended to give you a glimpse into what's needed to sell your home as a FSBO and help you decide whether it's right for your situation. If you decide to go this route, *The For Sale by Owner Kit* by Robert Irwin (Kaplan, 1998) is a helpful resource.

The sell-it-yourself route could be good for you in two situations:

1. You have substantial equity in your property and want to walk away with some of it.

2. You have little or no equity in your property and are afraid that your lender will come after you with a deficiency judgment if the sale doesn't produce enough money to pay off your mortgages. (See Chapter 10, "Face the Foreclosure Process," for details on deficiency judgments.) Therefore, you need to guard every penny, including those that would usually go to your real estate agent.

If you decide to go this route, be prepared for a lot of work and worry. People often complain that real estate agents don't do much for their commissions; you'll soon find out how wrong that is. In short, they help you with the three steps in a traditional home sale: preparation, offer, and closing. Figure 8.2 shows some of the tasks in each step.

Figure 8.2. *Home Sale Checklist*

Preparation

☐ Set sales price.

☐ Make a flyer to put in the "take one" box outside and give out at open houses.

☐ Take (or commission) good-quality photographs.

☐ List home in the local multiple-listing service, so area agents know about its availability.

☐ Advertise in the newspaper, local real-estate shoppers, etc.

☐ List home in other MLSs (such as national online databases).

☐ Acquire and fill out legally mandated forms, such as the transfer disclosure statement.

☐ Buy signs to display on the property itself and A-frame signs to put at nearby street corners when you're holding an open house.

☐ Pack up and remove clutter.

☐ Clean thoroughly.

☐ Perform repairs and improvements that will improve prospective buyers' first impressions.

☐ Order inspections that are either mandated by law or expected by local buyers.

(continued)

Figure 8.2. *Home Sale Checklist (continued)*

Offer

- ☐ Hold open houses.

- ☐ Meet with prospective buyers who can't attend open houses.

- ☐ Respond to inquiries by phone and email.

- ☐ Improve property based on visitors' observations.

- ☐ Manage offers.

- ☐ Make counteroffers (if necessary).

- ☐ Weed out "buyers" who can't perform.

Closing

- ☐ Manage backup offers (if appropriate).

- ☐ Deliver documents to the escrow officer or law firm.

- ☐ Continue negotiations during the escrow period (typically 20–60 days), including last-minute matters that could scuttle the deal.

- ☐ Review all legal forms.

- ☐ Work with escrow officers, attorneys, title companies, and other real estate professionals who make the sale possible.

- ☐ Ensure that all your issues are addressed at the closing table.

Local appears a lot in the checklist in Figure 8.2 because real estate is, first and foremost, a local business. Regulations and market expectations vary not only from state to state but from city to city—and, in some cities, from neighborhood to neighborhood. So no guide could possibly cover everything you need to know to equal the knowledge of an experienced local agent. Having said that, the question is this: Can an experienced local agent get you a price that's better than what you could do yourself, and will that difference be bigger than the commission? Sadly, there's no way to know. (The National Association of REALTORS®, which represents over 1 million real estate agents, claimed in a 2006 study that sellers who were represented by an agent got sales prices 16 percent higher on average than FSBO sellers. This study has come under scrutiny for its methodology, though.)

Which brings us to another matter: paying for the buyer's agent. In a traditional home sale, you hire a listing agent, who advertises the home's availability to other agents through the MLS. Part of that listing is a promise to pay a percentage of the sales price to the buyer's agent, who's also (confusingly) called the selling agent. That percentage is usually, but not always, half of the total commission. So although you as the seller might offer a 5 percent commission to sell your home, the listing agent only gets 2.5 percent, or even less. The selling agent receives the rest.

If you decide to sell your home yourself, you'll need to offer a commission to the buyer's agent to motivate that person to bring clients to your home. The percentage varies according to many factors, including location and sales price, but it's typically between 2 and 3 percent. You could forgo this expense by simply not offering your home through the local MLS and making clear to selling agents that you won't pay them any commission. But realize that, in doing so, you'll be cutting out a huge portion of your potential market, as the vast majority of homebuyers learn about the home they ultimately buy through their agents and are uncomfortable entering a transaction without their agent's guidance.

There are two other options besides using an agent and selling the home yourself. The first is a sort of hybrid real estate agency that's appeared over the past few years. Called discount brokers or fee-for-service brokers, such companies charge a set fee in exchange for guidance, forms, and access to agent-only services, such as the local MLS. However, you do the work of showing the home and negotiating with the seller. The big players in this field are Help-U-Sell (*www.helpusell.com*) and Assist-2-Sell (*www.assist2sell.com*), although sometimes a local brokerage will also offer à la carte services for sellers who only want partial service.

The other option is to sell your home through an auction site, such as eBay (*www.ebay.com*). To be honest, I've never heard of a seller's actually completing a deal satisfactorily this way. It appears that two types of people watch such real estate auctions: quick-sale buyers, who demand a large discount, and clueless beginners who are ultimately unable to follow through on the purchase. Having said that, the cost to list is low enough that it might be worth trying with a high reserve price so you don't have to take any offer you think is too low.

A number of websites advertise FSBO properties directly to the public. The issue here is this: Will prospective buyers see your ad? One way to find out is by checking the site's popularity on Alexa (*www.alexa.com*). Alexa rankings are given here for some of the better-known FSBO listing sites (December 2007; the lower the number, the better):

- RealtyTrac (*www.realtytrac.com*): ranking 14,163

- For Sale By Owner.com (*www.forsalebyowner.com*): ranking 24,397

- HomesByOwner.com (*www.homesbyowner.com*): ranking 84,386

- FSBO.com (*www.fsbo.com*): ranking 117,876

And of course, don't forget this one:

- Craigslist (*www.craigslist.org*): ranking 52. As Craigslist postings are both free and widely seen, this is a good place to try your first for-sale post.

Sell Using a Real Estate Agent

If selling your home yourself sounds like too much trouble, you won't have to look far to find a real estate agent who'll do the work for you in exchange for the commission. However, your situation is likely to be a bit different from what most agents are used to seeing. Here are some questions to make sure you choose one who's up to the task:

- Have you handled a property facing foreclosure before? How many have you handled?

- How much time do you believe will be needed to sell my home at our asking price? How long will it take to sell at 5 percent less? At 5 percent more?

- Have you ever negotiated with lenders for a short sale?

- What is your commission rate? How much of that will go to the seller's agent?

- What services are included? What expenses will you expect me to pay before closing (such as cleaning, staging, and the like)?

Some agents specialize in homes where the owners are facing financial difficulties: ask around to find one in your area. However, don't dismiss out of hand those who aren't as experienced in this area, if you feel they have other redeeming qualities. In my experience, some real estate "specialists," though knowledgeable, can become jaded from too much success in one area. Interview at least three agents to ensure that knowledge and experience is backed up by initiative, reliability, and communication skills.

Before meeting, give each agent details about the amount and description of every loan you want to be paid from the sale and ask for the agent to bring a seller's proceeds sheet along with a comparative market analysis to the meeting. If the agent doesn't have it—and I bet at least one of them won't—dismiss that person for not being able to follow instructions.

All real estate agents are licensed by the states in which they practice. In many states, you can look up licensing information—including any disciplinary actions—on the website of the department that administers real estate licenses in your state. (That's usually the secretary of state's department, but in any case, a Web search for "real estate license" and the name of your state should get you there.) Agents in every state have to undergo mandatory education and take a state test, the difficulty of which varies from state to state. Most states have two levels of agency, broker and salesperson (or terms to that effect). Brokers have undergone more education and are permitted to work solo. Salespeople must work under the supervision of a broker: technically speaking, the salesperson's supervising broker is your "agent."

Although people often use the two terms interchangeably, not every agent is a REALTOR®. To become a REALTOR®, an agent must join the National Association of REALTORS® (NAR), a private organization with over 1 million members. Local branches of the NAR usually control the MLS; therefore, to reach other agents effectively in most markets, one must be a REALTOR®.

The agent you choose will have you sign a listing agreement, which spells out not only the listing price and commission but also such matters as the length of the agreement and whether signs may be posted on the property. The agreement states that the agent is entitled to the commission if a "ready, willing, and able" buyer is produced, meaning that, even if your aunt decides to buy the house or you decide not to sell, you'll still owe the commission. When you sign a listing agreement, it's a true and solid commitment on your part. Which is fair, when you think about it: the agent puts in the work regardless.

As with the "Sell Your Home Yourself" section above, this book isn't big enough to discuss all the ins and outs of selling with an agent. For more information, *Kiplinger's Buying and Selling a Home: Make the Right Choice in Any Market* (2006, Kaplan) is a useful resource.

Move Forward

The sale process is a tremendous relief for a lot of people facing foreclosure—as long as the sale actually solves their problems. But what if you have other debts on top of your mortgage and can't reasonably work your way out of them? Then bankruptcy could be your answer. In fact, you may even be able to keep your home through some sorts of bankruptcy.

The next chapter, about bankruptcy, is the last one before discussing actual foreclosure. Its placement suggests that bankruptcy is a last-ditch option. Indeed, bankruptcy should not be taken lightly: you damage your credit, lose a tremendous amount of power to decide your own fate, and might not be able to keep your home when it's all done. But bankruptcy is designed not to punish debtors or curtail their ability to live. Rather, it provides structure and guidance that give many people great hope and that aren't available through any other means. Now more than ever, remember Essential Truth #5: You'll have to face difficult realizations and make difficult decisions—but you will survive.

If All Else Fails . . .
Declare Bankruptcy

Over 800,000 people filed for bankruptcy in the United States in 2007, and we can expect that number to increase as housing prices stagnate and credit becomes harder to obtain. At the same time, Congress recently enacted the Bankruptcy Abuse Prevention and Consumer Protection Act (BAPCPA), which makes it harder for some people to file for one type of bankruptcy. Reading the news can make you feel as though you're damned if you do and damned if you don't. Can bankruptcy still help financially troubled Americans save their homes?

The answer is a qualified yes. There are actually two kinds of bankruptcy available to most homeowners, commonly called Chapter 7 and Chapter 13 after their respective sections of federal law (Title 11, U.S. Code). Both are administered by the federal court system, which will appoint a trustee—typically an attorney or businessperson with substantial financial management experience—to oversee the process on a day-to-day basis.

- *Chapter 7.* Chapter 7 is a liquidation bankruptcy, where a court-appointed trustee can sell off all your valuable, nonexempt possessions to pay back the people you owe money—your creditors. In return, you're granted certain protections, including the right to protect a small amount of your home's equity through a homestead exemption in some circumstances. However, you're unlikely to be able to keep your home through a Chapter 7 bankruptcy.

- *Chapter 13.* Chapter 13 doesn't wipe your slate clean as Chapter 7 (mostly) does. Rather, you and the trustee work out a reorganization plan to repay your creditors as much as possible within three years (five for higher-income applicants). In exchange, you get to keep your possessions—as long as you fulfill your obligations under the repayment plan.

You can convert from one form of bankruptcy to the other if it becomes clear that the current one won't work. In fact, some debtors use a strategy called "Chapter 20" in which they first file for Chapter 7 for its advantages, then file for Chapter 13 for its different advantages. We won't discuss such tricks, both because they're advanced topics and because they're unlikely to help you keep your home.

Other forms of bankruptcy exist besides Chapters 7 and 13, but they're less likely to be of use to the average homeowner. Chapter 11 is primarily for businesses, although it's also available to people with extremely high debts (unsecured debts of at least $336,900 or secured debts of at least $1,010,650). Chapter 12 is for family farms, Chapter 15 is for unusual cases, and Chapter 9 is—believe it or not—for municipalities, such as city governments.

Even if you don't intend to go through with the full bankruptcy, filing could help you if you have a real plan for solving your problem but just need a little time, as it can stave off creditors for a few weeks before you dismiss it. This is tricky, though, and should not be done without the advice of a bankruptcy attorney.

As with Chapter 8, "Sell Before the Pain Starts," this book is too short to give much more than an overview of relevant bankruptcy possibilities. It aims instead only to help you decide whether they might be worth pursuing in your situation. *The Bankruptcy Handbook: Everything You Need to Know to Avoid Bankruptcy, Get Rid of Debt, and Rebuild Your Credit* (2008, Kaplan) and *The Bankruptcy Kit* (2004, Kaplan), both by John Ventura, are full-length works on the subject.

Basic Rules for Bankruptcy

The simplistic view of bankruptcy is that you go in, they take everything away, and you walk out with a clean slate: no possessions, no debts. But the reality—even in "straight" Chapter 7 bankruptcies—is more nuanced.

1. *You have to give up any idea that you'll have control of the process.* Declaring bankruptcy is a lot like facing the first 3 steps of a traditional 12-step program: you're declaring that you're powerless over your finances; believe that a power greater than yourself—the court, in this case—can restore you; and have decided to turn over your will and life to that greater power. Bankruptcy is a harsh master, and if you mess up, the courts will throw you to the wolves—that is, back into the hands of your creditors.

2. *Bankruptcy can't make an unprofitable life profitable.* Remember Essential Truth #1: You can't beat math. If your non-debt expenses exceeded your income before bankruptcy, the same will be true after bankruptcy.

3. *You will substantially lose financial ability.* Americans have come to see the availability of easy credit as a right; bankruptcy shows you, day by day, that that's not true. Suddenly, you won't be able to get loans, buy a new car, or finance a business—at least, not with reasonable terms. If you do get loans (from a lender specializing in bankruptcy cases), they'll be only with the permission of the bankruptcy court and under the worst terms possible. Get yourself back into debt trouble again, and you're barred from filing from bankruptcy again for several years. And your bankruptcy remains on your credit report for *10 years.*

Regardless of whether you file for Chapter 7 or Chapter 13, you'll need to undergo a credit-counseling program, details of which are from the Department of Justice (*www.usdoj.gov/ust/eo/bap-cpa/ccde*). However, if you received a certificate from undergoing credit counseling after following the advice in Chapter 5, "Call for Help," you may have already completed this step.

For bankruptcy purposes, all debts are divided into three categories:

■ *Priority debts.* Priority debts can't be discharged—that is, removed from your pile of debt. You're going to pay these no matter what, unless you work out an arrangement directly with the creditor. Income and property taxes are in this category, as are child support payments, alimony, and money you owe to employees. Judgment debts that were incurred because of malice or fraud are also considered priority debts.

- *Secured debts.* Secured debts are those that have a lien on something you own—that is, the lender has the right to repossess it if you fail to pay the debt. Mortgages and car loans are the big items in this category.

- *Unsecured debts.* Unsecured debts comprise debts that are secured only by your good faith. If you fail to pay these, the most a lender can do is pursue collection and possibly sue you for repayment. These include credit cards, medical and legal bills, and most court judgments.

Regardless of your situation, filing for bankruptcy immediately puts an automatic stay on your creditors' attempts to collect money from you: after you tell them about the filing, the phone calls and bills simply stop, and they stay stopped as long as you're in bankruptcy proceedings, which could last as little as 15 days (if you fail to file follow-up papers) or as long as years (if you enter reorganization). Foreclosure proceedings also stop, although your lender can file a "motion for relief from an automatic stay," which the judge can grant if you fail to perform on any part of your reorganization plan. (Once again, the wolves.)

Needless to say, bankruptcy filings require a lot of paperwork—much of which you'll have at hand if you followed recommendations outlined in Chapter 2, "Get a Handle on Your Situation." Court filing fees will be several hundred dollars, although you may be able to get out of paying those by filing a fee waiver, and attorney's fees could run into thousands of dollars. You *can* manage your own bankruptcy, and many people do. But if any of your creditors contests your plans, you may quickly find yourself in over your head. At the very least, contact your local Bar Association through the directory at *www.abanet.org/legalservices/findlegalhelp/home. cfm*. Many bar associations have a program that sets up a low-cost "check-'em-out" appointment with an attorney near you.

Chapter 13 Bankruptcy

The idea behind Chapter 13 bankruptcy is to lighten your debt load and get creditors off your back while you work your way out of a hole. If you qualify, you'll work out a plan to repay as much debt as possible for three years, or five years if you're above the median income level for your area. At the end of that time, the remainder of your debt *might* be wiped out, although the judge can grant a creditor's request for it to remain. So don't automatically expect to get your newly bought house for free when the three years are up!

Generally speaking, the main criterion to qualify for Chapter 13 bankruptcy is that you can demonstrate a reasonable expectation of a stable income for the next few years, high enough to meet your payment plan's requirements. The court-appointed trustee will look over your plan, ensure that you'll dedicate all your disposable income to repayment of debt, advise you on how to make the plan more workable, and submit recommendations to the court. From then on, you'll pay the money you owe and an administrative fee to that trustee, who in turn will forward payments to your creditors.

While you're in Chapter 13 bankruptcy, your trustee is like your parents. You have to make an annual report, show that you've continued to pay for such things as taxes and child support, and, of course, make your monthly payment. If your financial situation changes, you must go to your trustee to figure out how that affects the bankruptcy. Ultimately, the trustee is the only witness to your good faith, and the court will believe testimony from that source.

Chapter 7 Bankruptcy

Chapter 7 bankruptcy is usually not the best choice for someone facing foreclosure, because the court will order your home sold to pay off creditors if it has any equity in it. If it doesn't have any equity, the lender will probably be permitted to just go ahead with foreclosure in any case, as that's the best chance at recapturing the money it loaned you. Having said that, filing for Chapter 7 bankruptcy will buy you some time while the trustee and court are deciding what to do with your property.

So when would a homeowner use Chapter 7 bankruptcy? Primarily when you know you're going to lose the home anyway, don't have sufficient income to justify a Chapter 13 reorganization plan, and want other debts discharged as well. Further, some of your equity might be protected in Chapter 7 bankruptcy through your claim of a homestead exemption. But we're not talking about a lot of money: the federal exemption amount is currently $18,450, while in some states, it's even less. In states with an exemption below $18,450, it makes sense to claim the federal exemption amount. A state-by-state guide to homestead exemptions is at *www.assetprotectionbook.com/ homestead_exemptions.htm.*

Move Forward

At this point, we've looked at every avenue for handling your problem except for the one, big, looming one: foreclosure. But even that doesn't have to be so bad—if it's handled thoughtfully, intelligently, and honestly. The next chapter will show you how to make it as painless as possible.

10

Face the Foreclosure
Process

For you, the foreclosure procedure is a major event. It might represent the culmination of years of striving against odds and coming up short, or it might be the result of a sudden, unexpected event. Or it might be a welcome relief that frees your spirit and allows you to move on to life's next stage. But for the legal, financial, and real estate professionals involved, foreclosures are a fairly routine matter. Some of them handle dozens of foreclosures a year, but even those who are involved in only one or two are unlikely to be as frightened, confused, or emotionally involved as you are.

On one hand, their lack of passion can feel jarring, even insulting. But on the other, the fact that yours is just one file in a stack can be reassuring. They've been through this many times before and seen other people come through the foreclosure process strong and whole. Some who have been in the business long enough can even tell tales of a foreclosed party coming back years later to buy another home—and prosper in it.

I encourage you to take comfort in this wisdom and remember not to take their seeming lack of caring personally—because they certainly don't. Instead, read this chapter to gain the knowledge that will allow you to go through the process knowledgeably, unaffected by the confusion that could cloud your judgment.

Make a Foreclosure Calendar: Judicial Foreclosure

The foreclosure process is ruled by state law and varies tremendously from state to state. As a result, this book couldn't hope to cover all the ins and outs of specific state laws. But basically, foreclosure procedures are divided into two categories: judicial and nonjudicial.

In either case, the first couple of steps, which mark the start of the preforeclosure period, are the same:

1. *Day 1.* You're late on a payment. The lender starts charging you fees according to your loan agreement, typically 15 days after the payment was due.

2. *Days 30–45.* The lender sends you a borrower information packet, giving the current status of your loan, how much it would cost (including fees) to bring it back up to date, a booklet from HUD entitled "How to Avoid Foreclosure" (also downloadable from *www.hud.gov/foreclosure/*), and a phone number to call to discuss any problems.

3. *Days 46–90.* Continued communications come from your lender, which can decide at any time to start the foreclosure proceedings. Lenders will generally wait for at least a couple of months of missed payments before turning on the heat.

From here, the procedures differ somewhat. Judicial foreclosures are generally required when you have a mortgage rather than a deed of trust, unless the mortgage includes a power-of-sale clause. (See Chapter 6, "Understand Your Loan," for an explanation of the difference.) In many states, the lender with a deed of trust (or mortgage with a power-of-sale clause) also has the option to start a judicial foreclosure if it chooses. Here's the basic process:

1. The lender initiates a lawsuit (or "suit") by filing a complaint with the court, which you receive by mail.

2. The lender records a document called a *lis pendens* (Latin for "lawsuit in progress") with the county government. This tells the world about the lawsuit through constructive notice—that is, the information isn't distributed, but anyone who bothers to look at the public record of your home's file will learn about the suit. Other prospective lenders and purchasers would look at that file before completing a deal, so the lis pendens makes it much harder to sell or refinance your home without your existing lender's involvement.

3. You have to file a response to the lender's lawsuit, typically within 30 days, in which you announce your intention to contest the suit and correct any errors in it. If you don't file a response, the court can (and, in fact, is likely to) assume that the lender's complaint is completely correct and true and simply award it a full judgment. If that happens, you'll have a hard time trying to get the case open again. So even if you agree with everything the lender says, file a response!

4. If you disagree with points on the lender's lawsuit—and your response says so—there will be a trial to determine the truth. The trial could take anywhere from a day to several years, depending on the complexity of the case and the strength of the competing arguments.

5. Throughout this process, you can still reinstate the loan by paying everything you owe, plus fees and costs. Whatever you do, continue to treat the property as your home by paying bills, performing maintenance, and occupying the home. If it appears that you've moved out, the lender could say you abandoned the property, which could harm your position in court.

6. Regardless of whether you contest the lawsuit, eventually the judge will make a judgment and record it with the county government. For the sake of this narrative, we'll assume that the judge found the lender's claims to be substantially true: it made you a loan secured by your home, you failed to pay it back according to the terms, and the lender has the right to repossess your home. The lender is now known as the judgment creditor; you are the judgment debtor.

An appeal might be possible at this point if you believe there was a defect in how the case was tried, but now we're getting well into the realm of advanced law and well beyond what is typical in simple foreclosure cases. If you want to pursue this unlikely avenue, consult with a local attorney.

7. At this time, you still have the right of redemption—that is, you can get your home back by paying off the entire loan, plus all fees and costs (including court costs for the foreclosure procedure thus far). That's going to be more difficult now, of course, because any lender you approach for a refinance will see from the public record that the home is the subject of a lawsuit.

8. The judge files a writ of sale, which explicitly confirms that your home may be sold by the court to satisfy the debt, and (in some places) a notice of levy, which directs the sheriff to enforce the judgment.

9. You'll now receive a notice of sale (NOS), providing details on when and where your home will be offered for sale. The sale typically takes place 30–90 days after the notice has been delivered. Complicated rules govern how this and other notices are delivered. For example, local law may require that it be mailed to you, taped to your front door, and mailed to all your tenants. (If you can show that notice wasn't given according to the letter of the law, you might be able to delay—but not defeat—foreclosure at this point.)

In addition, the notice will be published in a "newspaper of general circulation," typically a daily or weekly that's set up to print such notices and is widely available in the area where your property is located. In most states, the ad needs to run for three or four weeks, although it could be as little as seven days (in Minnesota) or as long as six months (in Indiana). Such publications are eagerly tracked by investors who specialize in buying foreclosed homes, and the notices are reproduced many places online, such as *www.realtytrac.com* and *www.foreclosures.com*.

10. The sale date arrives, and with it the foreclosure sale (or, as it's sometimes known, sheriff's sale). The sheriff appears at the appointed place—usually the front steps of city hall or the courthouse—and reads the legally required notices, including terms of the sale. Then the bidding begins. The sheriff starts it off by providing a bid from your lender for the amount of the loan or the value of the home, whichever is less. (Obviously, the lender wouldn't end up paying itself that amount: it would be a "paper" transaction, whereby it simply took the property and either extinguished the debt or filed for a deficiency judgment if the bid was smaller than the loan—see below.)

Besides bids from individual investors, you're likely to see some from junior lienholders—that is, other parties whom you owe money through a loan secured by your home. Let's say, for example, that your home has a market value of $400,000 and is secured by a $300,000 first loan (which is foreclosing) and a $50,000 second loan. If it goes for less than $350,000 plus costs and fees, that will come out of the second lender's payment: it will only get the remainder, even if it's less than $50,000—or nothing. Therefore, the lender who holds the second loan might bid $350,000. Even though it doesn't want the trouble of owning (and reselling) the home, that's a better option than facing the potential loss of its entire $50,000 loan amount.

When the winning bid has been called, the sheriff declares the home sold, takes payment (most foreclosure sales require immediate payment in full), issues the winning buyer a certificate of sale, and heads back to the office to pay off all the loans secured by your (former) home. First costs of the sale are paid off, followed by property taxes, followed by all liens in the order in which they were recorded. The rules for priority of liens can actually get a bit complicated; understanding them isn't of much importance to you, the former owner of the foreclosed home. The most important thing to know is that, if there's any money left over after all these people have been paid off, you get it. So hope for a high sale price!

What if you owe the foreclosing lender $300,000 and the winning bid (after expenses) is only for $250,000? Bad news, I'm afraid. If the law allows and procedures were followed properly, the lender can choose to pursue a deficiency judgment for the full amount of $50,000. Surprisingly, many lenders don't. If you don't have other property or major assets, they realize that they "can't get blood from a stone," and there's little chance you'll be able to pay them.

In states where the lender can choose to pursue either judicial or nonjudicial foreclosures, the promise of a deficiency judgment is the main reason they choose the more expensive and time-consuming judicial path. Deficiency judgments aren't permitted in nonjudicial foreclosures, where the lender simply exercises its power of sale.

But wait, it's not over yet! Many states continue to give you, the former homeowner, a right of redemption period *after* the sale. Let's say that you suddenly inherit a large sum of money and want to buy the home back. You—and, in most states, only you—can redeem the property by giving the court the amount paid by the foreclosure purchaser, plus all costs (including interest). In return, you get the property back. (A redemption differs from a reinstatement in that a reinstatement continues your old loan as before, while redemption doesn't.) However, this process doesn't wipe out any deficiency judgment; you could still owe your old lender money after buying back the property.

Surprisingly, you're still allowed to live in the home during this redemption period, often as long as a year and even two years in Tennessee. (The period may vary depending on whether there was a deficiency judgment.) However, you have to pay rent to the new owner, and it also gets any other income the property produces, for example rent you used to collect for the garage space.

If you don't redeem the property during the redemption period, the new owner is issued a sheriff's deed, and you have no further claims on the property. Unless you start a standard rental agreement with the new owner, you have to move out at this point.

The right of redemption can be sold in some states and can be transferred by contract in those states where that's not directly possible. If you had substantial equity in your home or if it appreciates during the redemption period, investors who can afford to buy back the home at "your" price will be interested in paying you for this right. These are known as postforeclosure sales. For example, let's say your home had a $300,000 market value when it was sold at foreclosure and you have the right to redeem it for $280,000. Due to a large employer's setting up shop in town, your home could now fetch $350,000 on the open market. An investor might pay you $20,000 for your right of redemption. The investor will then use that right to buy your old home from the foreclosure purchaser at $280,000. After spending $300,000 in total, the investor resells the home at $350,000, making $50,000 profit. Nice work if you can finance it!

Make a Foreclosure Calendar: Nonjudicial Foreclosure

Nonjudicial foreclosures under a power-of-sale clause are considerably simpler, as no courts are involved. The preforeclosure period is generally the same as in judicial foreclosures. You miss some payments, and there's some communication between you and the lender before it decides to start the foreclosure process. But from there, significant differences arise.

1. The nonjudicial foreclosure starts when the lender directs the trustee to prepare a notice of default (NOD), sometimes more formally called a notice of default and election to sell. As with many other legal documents, the trustee must follow very specific rules regarding how the NOD is recorded and delivered to you and others with an interest in

your property (such as tenants and other lienholders). The trustee might be required to publish the NOD in a local general-circulation newspaper, although this requirement isn't as pervasive as for some other documents. (As always, check the laws in your state.)

2. A mandatory reinstatement period begins, during which you have the right to defeat the foreclosure by paying all the money you owe, plus fees and costs. At this point, a junior lienholder, such as the company that holds your second mortgage, can reinstate your first loan by paying the money you owe. It would then add that repaid amount to the junior lien and begin foreclosing the second mortgage if you don't immediately repay the money advanced to cover the first loan.

3. If you don't reinstate your loan by the time the reinstatement period is over, the trustee files a notice of trustee's sale, also known by the same *notice of sale* term used for a judicial foreclosure. Again, the trustee has to deliver and publish this notice according to detailed rules. In some states, you still have rights of reinstatement during this period.

4. Ultimately, the property is sold through a trustee's sale, which looks exactly like a sheriff-run foreclosure sale, except that it's performed by a representative for the trustee. The rules are read, the bidding takes place, and the proceeds are disbursed in basically the same way as in a judicial foreclosure.

The three big differences between a judicial and nonjudicial foreclosure are as follows:

1. *The new buyer receives a trustee's deed.* A trustee's deed is an outright, immediate deed to the property.

2. *You have no right of redemption.* You lose all rights to the property as soon as the new owner's deed is delivered to the buyer and must either move out or pay rent as the new owner requires.

3. *The lender can't come after you for a deficiency judgment.* As soon as the nonjudicial sale is over, you're free of the foreclosed debt!

Get Details of Your State's Foreclosure Procedures

You'll notice that in both judicial and nonjudicial foreclosures, your "opponent" (whether the lender or a trustee) has to follow some very specific procedures. Therein lies an opportunity for you to defeat the foreclosure: if you can show the other party did something wrong, it may have to start from the beginning again. That only buys you time, of course—but in cases where time is all you need, your opponent's errors could be your saving grace.

These procedures are largely ruled by state law with some minor variations from county to county. (In extremely rare cases, a lender may foreclose in federal court, where the rules are different.) A brief state-by-state list of state laws is given in Figure 10.1, but details on such technical matters as notice, liability, court procedure, and the like are well beyond what can be covered here. The following websites provide much more detail on the laws of individual states:

- *www.realtytrac.com/foreclosure_laws_overview.asp*
- *www.stopping-banks-foreclosures.com/state-foreclosure-process.html*

- *http://stopforeclosure.com/Foreclosure_Laws.htm*

- *www.law.cornell.edu/wex/index.php/Mortgage/*

These laws could potentially change at any time: I recommend you take a look at the states' official websites listed below and contact a local attorney to confirm points of concern. After each state's name, this list shows the following information:

- Whether the lender can follow judicial foreclosure, nonjudicial foreclosure, or both and which is more common

- Total time between the filing of the notice of default and the sale date

- The typical number of days (if any) after the sale that you're allowed to redeem the property

- The state's official legislative website, where (with some digging) you'll find the actual texts of relevant laws

Move Forward

A hundred and thirty years ago the painter James McNeill Whistler sued critic John Ruskin for what he felt were libelous comments Ruskin had made about one of his paintings. On the stand, Ruskin's attorney noted that Whistler had completed the painting in a very short time and asked, "The labour of two days ... is that for which you ask two hundred guineas?" Whistler responded, "No, I ask it for the knowledge of a lifetime."

The point Whistler made is true for you today: the experience you've gained through the foreclosure process will serve you in unexpected ways, when a moment's decision will be informed by

Figure 10.1. *State-by-State Guide to Foreclosure Processes*

Alabama. Nonjudicial preferred, judicial permitted. 49–74 days. Redemption possible for 365 days. *www.legislature.state.al.us*

Alaska. Nonjudicial preferred, judicial permitted. 105 days. Redemption possible for 365 days (judicial foreclosures only). *www.legis.state.ak.us*

Arizona. Nonjudicial preferred, judicial permitted. 90+ days. Redemption possible for 30–180 days (judicial foreclosures only). *www.azleg.gov*

Arkansas. Judicial or nonjudicial, used equally. 70 days. Redemption possible for 365 days (judicial foreclosures only). *www.arkleg.state.ar.us*

California. Nonjudicial preferred, judicial permitted. 117 days. Redemption possible for 365 days (judicial foreclosures only). *www.leginfo.ca.gov*

Colorado. Nonjudicial preferred, judicial permitted. 91 days. Redemption possible for 75 days. *www.leg.state.co.us*

Connecticut. Judicial only. 62 days. Judge decides number of days redemption is possible. *www.cga.ct.gov*

Delaware. Judicial only. 170–210 days. No redemption possible. *http://legis.delaware.gov*

District of Columbia. Nonjudicial only. 47 days. No redemption possible. *www.dccouncil.washington.dc.us*

Florida. Judicial only. 135 days. No redemption possible. *www.flsenate.gov/statutes*

Georgia. Nonjudicial preferred, judicial permitted. 37 days. No redemption possible. *www.legis.state.ga.us*

Figure 10.1. *State-by-State Guide to Foreclosure Processes (continued)*

Hawaii. Judicial or nonjudicial, used equally. 220 days. No redemption possible. *www.capitol.hawaii.gov*

Idaho. Nonjudicial preferred, judicial permitted. 150 days. Redemption possible for 365 days. *www.legislature.idaho.gov*

Illinois. Judicial only. 300 days. Redemption possible for 90 days. *www.legislature.idaho.gov*

Indiana. Judicial only. 261 days. No redemption possible. *www.in.gov/legislative*

Iowa. Judicial or nonjudicial. 160 days. Redemption possible for 20 days. *www.legis.state.ia.us*

Kansas. Judicial only. 130 days. Redemption possible for 365 days. *www.kslegislature.org*

Kentucky. Judicial only. 147 days. Redemption possible for 365 days. *www.lrc.state.ky.us*

Louisiana. Judicial only. 180 days. No redemption possible. *www.louisiana.gov*

Maine. Judicial only. 240 days. Redemption possible for 90 days. *http://janus.state.me.us/legis/*

Maryland. Judicial only. 46 days. Judge decides number of days redemption is possible. *www.mlis.state.md.us*

Massachusetts. Judicial only. 75 days. No redemption possible. *www.mass.gov/legis/*

Michigan. Nonjudicial only. 60 days. Redemption possible for 30–365 days. *www.legislature.mi.gov*

(continued)

Figure 10.1. *State-by-State Guide to Foreclosure Processes (continued)*

Minnesota. Nonjudicial preferred, judicial permitted. 90–100 days. Redemption possible for 365 days. *www.leg.state.mn.us*

Mississippi. Nonjudicial preferred, judicial permitted. 90 days. No redemption possible. *www.ls.state.ms.us*

Missouri. Nonjudicial preferred, judicial permitted. 60 days. Redemption possible for 365 days. *www.moga.state.mo.us*

Montana. Nonjudicial preferred, judicial permitted. 150 days. No redemption possible. *http://leg.mt.gov*

Nebraska. Judicial only. 142 days. No redemption possible. *www.nebraskalegislature.gov*

Nevada. Judicial or nonjudicial. 116 days. No redemption possible. *www.leg.state.nv.us*

New Hampshire. Nonjudicial only. 59 days. No redemption possible. *www.gencourt.state.nh.us/ns/*

New Jersey. Judicial only. 270 days. Redemption possible for 10 days. *www.gencourt.state.nh.us/ns/*

New Mexico. Judicial only. 180 days. Redemption possible for 30–270 days. *http://legis.state.nm.us/lcs/*

New York. Judicial only. 445 days. No redemption possible. *www.assembly.state.ny.us*

North Carolina. Nonjudicial preferred, judicial permitted. 110 days. No redemption possible. *www.ncga.state.nc.us*

North Dakota. Judicial only. 150 days. Redemption possible for 180–365 days. *www.legis.nd.gov*

Figure 10.1. *State-by-State Guide to Foreclosure Processes (continued)*

Ohio. Judicial only. 217 days. No redemption possible. *www. legislature.state.oh.us*

Oklahoma. Judicial preferred, nonjudicial permitted. 186 days. No redemption possible. *www.lsb.state.ok.us*

Oregon. Nonjudicial preferred, judicial permitted. 150 days. Redemption possible for 180 days. *www.leg.state.or.us*

Pennsylvania. Judicial only. 270 days. No redemption possible. *www.legis.state.pa.us*

Rhode Island. Nonjudicial preferred, judicial permitted. 62 days. No redemption possible. *www.rilin.state.ri.us*

South Carolina. Judicial only. 150 days. No redemption possible. *www.scstatehouse.net*

South Dakota. Judicial preferred, nonjudicial permitted. 150 days. Redemption possible for 30–365 days. *www.legis.state.sd.us*

Tennessee. Nonjudicial only. 40–45 days. Redemption possible for 730 days. *www.legislature.state.tn.us*

Texas. Nonjudicial preferred, judicial permitted. 27 days. No redemption possible. *www.capitol.state.tx.us*

Utah. Judicial only. 142 days. Judge decides number of days redemption is possible. *www.le.state.ut.us*

Vermont. Judicial only. 95 days. Redemption possible for 180–365 days. *www.leg.state.vt.us*

Virginia. Nonjudicial preferred, judicial permitted. 45 days. No redemption possible. *www.virginia.gov*

(continued)

Figure 10.1. *State-by-State Guide to Foreclosure Processes (continued)*

Washington. Nonjudicial preferred, judicial permitted. 135 days. No redemption possible. *www.leg.wa.gov*

West Virginia. Nonjudicial only. 60–90 days. No redemption possible. *www.legis.state.wv.us*

Wisconsin. Judicial preferred, nonjudicial permitted. 290 days. Redemption possible for 365 days. *www.legis.state.wi.us*

Wyoming. Nonjudicial preferred, judicial permitted. 60 days. Redemption possible for 90–365 days. *http://legisweb.state.wy.us*

---

the good and bad you've lived through in managing the revival (or disposal) of your home. You have added to your knowledge of a lifetime; payment awaits at the moment that capitalizes on that experience.

No matter what the outcome of your situation has been, congratulations on reaching the end of this book. You are now better educated than 90 percent of all homeowners and in an outstanding position to move forward. I hope you'll be able to fully profit from your newfound knowledge, and look forward to hearing about your successes online at *www.savemyhomebook.com.*

Index